Blue Milk and Green Water

Annette Zoheret

Copyright © 2015 Annette Zoheret
All rights reserved.

*I dedicate this book to my wonderful family in gratitude for our many happy memories.
I love you all!*

Contents

Introduction 1
The Third One Really Stirs the Pot 3
Pet Rescue 7
Whispering Spirits 17
Stink and Think 31
The Untold Tale 35
Puppy Obedience 43
The Hilton Hotel 45
The Mouse Days of Winter 51
The Perfect Christmas Tree 57
Grand Bahama Island 71
Ostara 95
Family Reunion 99
Blue Milk and Green Water 105
Hero 111
My Royal Experience 117
The Hornet 127
The 13th Wedding Anniversary 131
The Backyard Construction Project 141
Head over Heels 145
Epilogue and Acknowledgments 149

My husband Pieter went to the pet store to purchase some hay for our rabbit.

The sales rep smiled at him.

"You have a pet bunny?" she asked.

"Actually, we have a food chain: dog, cat, ferret, bunny, bird, and guinea pig."

She nodded knowingly. "Oh, you've got kids!"

Introduction

The stories in this book originated as e-mails to my friends, usually after pandemonium had struck my house – and it seemed to strike a lot.

Apparently, I am to blame for coffee stains on computer screens when unleashing one of my family's adventures without first issuing a coffee-spit warning.

In response to many requests for the book, I've compiled a series of stories spanning some fifteen years. Most of these memories are funny, some are sad, but all are true.

Oh, and some names have been changed to protect the not-so-innocent.

Please keep a tissue box handy. I won't accept further responsibility for spit damage.

Enjoy!

The Third One Really Stirs the Pot

As the mother of two girls, I thought I was well prepared to have another. But one of my relatives, who already had three girls, had warned me.
"Watch out! The third one really stirs the pot."
Of course, I didn't listen. How bad could it be?

Nadia was born with fluid in her lungs and an intestinal streptococcal infection. I spent the first two days watching my poor baby lying in an incubator hooked up to tubes and wires, praying she would see another day; hence the name Nadia, a Russian name which means hope.

What doesn't kill you makes you stronger, and Nadia was strong—willed, that is.
I should have known we were in trouble when her horoscope predicted she would grow up to become either the leader of a country or motorcycle gang.

When she was three years old, we had one of our many interesting conversation at the dinner table.
"Mom, why do you and Dad always make the rules? Why can't we kids make rules, too?" Maya, aged eight, asked.
"Yeah," chimed in Lucia, all of six years old. "We want to make rules too!"

"Okay," I said. "We'll start with the youngest member of the family. Nadia, if you could make a rule, what would it be?"

She stood straight up, bristling with importance, her tiny finger pointing up the stairs.

"Maya! Lucy! Go clean my room!"

That didn't endear her much to her sisters. Shortly thereafter, Maya convinced her to stick a crayon up her nose. My mother was babysitting for me that evening while I attended a sewing class, and Pieter worked a night shift at the hospital. It quickly became clear that the slowly melting crayon couldn't be removed with a good blow into a tissue, so my mother and daughters trooped off to the hospital.

When my husband arrived in the emergency department, two doctors and a number of nurses had assembled around his youngest child.

"Hi, Dad! I got crayon up my nose!" Nadia announced happily.

It took several attempts and various pointy instruments to remove the mushy piece of crayon. The event also earned her the nickname "Crayola" at the hospital.

Little Nadia knew no fear, and there were times when I wondered if she would ever see the ripe old age of ten. She had the uncanny ability to find alternative uses for toys deemed safe by toy advisory boards.

One morning, she had gone outside with her skipping rope, and I had undressed to take a hasty shower. There was a knock on my door by a well-meaning neighbor who informed me that my youngest was busy hanging herself in the driveway. I rushed outside in my nightgown to find Nadia hanging in her skipping rope, which she had looped through the basketball net.

"Nadia! What are you doing?"

"I'm playing torture!" Undoubtedly a game taught to her by Maya.

I ushered her into the backyard and told her not to wrap the skipping rope around anything else.

"The skipping rope is for skipping only!"

I went back inside and took up my lookout post by the kitchen window. Sure enough, she immediately busied herself with wrapping the skipping rope around a tree branch. Out I went again.

"Nadia, what did Mommy say?"

"Skip rope."

"Right! Don't wrap the rope around anything else. You could get hurt!"

"Yes, Mommy."

"If you wrap the rope around anything else, Mommy will take it away!"

Why do we speak of ourselves in the third person when we talk to our kids?

I went back inside and returned to the kitchen window. There was no hesitation. Nadia took the rope to the picket fence surrounding her tree house, which was five feet above ground. This time, I confiscated the rope and replaced it with some nice, safe sidewalk chalk.

"Here, Nadia, why don't you color our patio and make it look nice?"

"Okay, Mommy."

Fearing no evil, I went inside and took one last look through my observatory. She sat back on her haunches, picking a piece of chalk. Now was my big chance for a five-minute shower. What could she possibly do with sidewalk chalk? It was too big to shove up her nose, and she couldn't possibly hang herself with it.

Never say never.

The minute I got out of the shower, I went back to the kitchen window. There was my child with every psychedelic color imaginable running down her front. She spat out sidewalk chalk she had mixed to a pulp with her saliva, spreading it over the patio by dancing barefoot through the mixture and leaving tiny colorful footprints.

Did I mention she was wearing her Sunday best? We were ready to go out as soon as Mommy had showered and changed.

Pet Rescue

My mother called me in high excitement. She had been feeding a stray cat that had rewarded her efforts by producing a litter of kittens under the back porch. Since I had spent many childhood days taming wild barn cats, my mother hoped that I could work my magic on her porch residents.

Although mama cat was somewhat tame, her offspring were anything but. All my attempts failed miserably, and we were running out of time. The leaves were turning and there was a nip in the night air.

I called the Humane Society who informed me it was "kitten season" and they were full. Furthermore, they didn't come out to people's houses to trap cats. However, they did put me in touch with a local volunteer group called Pet Rescue who was willing to lend me a live trap.

I coaxed mama cat into a carrier then placed the carrier and the trap, end to end, in the bushes. A while later, I had mother and four kittens safely ensconced in my laundry room.

Luckily, Pet Rescue found a foster home for mama almost

immediately, but that still left me with four wild kittens, hissing and spitting every time I came near. With patience and kitten food, I soon had them cuddling and litter trained, which meant Pet Rescue could find them new homes.

Around this time, Pieter was spending his fortieth birthday with his sister in Australia, leaving me with three young children, a dog, a house, a full-time job, and a laundry room full of kittens. It turned out to be the longest month of my life.

The fun started with the weather turning colder and freezing the pipe for the garden hose. I came home one evening to find my basement under water. No matter what I did, I was unable to turn off the tap to the broken pipe. Pieter's friend, Vern, was the recipient of my first SOS call. He arrived in his firefighter gear and turned off the tap with nothing but his bare hands. What can I say? Upper body strength was never the best part of my physical makeup. Furthermore, it was a treat to see a man in firefighter gear. (You know what they say about men in uniform.)

The next incident came in the form of a storm that dumped so much snow onto our backyard trees that one of them decided to surrender, effectively blocking the sidewalk. Luckily, City workers came and removed it.

Things usually come in threes, or so the saying goes, and I wondered what else could possibly go wrong. I didn't have to wait long. The kittens were now almost three months old, and the laundry room was no longer sufficient to occupy their growing curiosity. They became adept at climbing the baby gate that had halted their progress in the past. It was high time Pet Rescue found homes for them.

One fateful evening, the kitten named Tiggy left the laundry-room sanctuary and went exploring after everyone had gone to bed. At 2:00 a.m., I awoke to the sound of a kitten crying but couldn't place the source. Bleary-eyed, I reluctantly left my warm bed to find where the insistent meowing was coming from. A quick check confirmed that I was short one kitten. I followed the sound of the little voice into the living room. On all fours, I checked underneath the sofa and chairs and even looked in the fireplace. No Tiggy to be found, only his plaintive calling, which seemed to come up through the floor.

I descended the stairs into the still, damp basement, calling and searching to no avail. Then my eyes found the entrance to the crawlspace beneath the living room. Maybe he had mistaken this large, sand-filled space for a giant litter box. The thought discouraged me from crawling in there in the dead of night, especially since it had no light. I needed someone to hold up a flashlight for me.

As if on cue, my eldest daughter, Maya, appeared, barefoot and shivering.

"Mom, I hear a kitten meowing."

"I know, dear. I think Tiggy is stuck in the crawlspace and can't find his way out."

Maya agreed to hold the flashlight, and I reluctantly climbed through the small opening that led underneath the living room floor. I didn't get far. It was pitch black, and I could feel spider webs on my face. No way! Tiggy would have to stay there for the night.

I climbed back out and Maya shrieked. In my white nightgown, with spider webs caught in my hair, I must have been a scary sight in the flickering glow of the flashlight.

I brought her back to bed and tried my best to ignore Tiggy's frantic meowing. It made for a long night.

I greeted the next morning exhausted and filled with trepidation. I wasn't looking forward to another trip into the crawlspace. Tiggy had stopped crying, and I was concerned he might have met an untimely end.

My mother called to ask how I was coping without Pieter at home, and I told her. Shortly afterward, there was a knock on the door, and my mother's friend, John, stood in the doorway offering his help. He was more than welcome to explore the crawlspace on my behalf.

Equipped with a flashlight and a bowl of cat treats, he descended into the dark and emerged a short time later, draped in cobwebs and sprinkled with dust.

"No cat in there," he said, "but there's a hole in the back of the crawlspace that leads into the wall. I think your cat went up that way."

As if to prove his point, we heard Tiggy taking up his lament in the living room wall.

"What can we do? We can't leave him in there."

John batted at his clothes, trying to release the clinging cobwebs.

"Well, I left the cat food at the back of the crawlspace near the hole. He'll likely come down when he's hungry."

Pieter called shortly after John left.

"Hi, dear, how's it going?"

I told him how it was going and asked how he'd feel about my cutting holes into the newly renovated living room wall. There was a brief hesitation before I heard him sigh.

"Whatever you have to do to get that cat out of the wall is fine by me."

I went back into the living room and eyed the walls. The problem was I had no idea which wall Tiggy was hiding behind. I pictured my living-room walls looking like a golf course.

"Tiggy?" I called tentatively into the empty living room.

No reply.

Fear clutched at my heart. How long did it take before a

kitten became dehydrated? What if Tiggy died inside my living room wall? The stench— not to mention the trauma to the kids—unthinkable! I felt sick with worry.

There was no sign of life from Tiggy until late in the afternoon when I went upstairs to my bedroom and stopped dead in my tracks. I heard an odd sound emanating from the door frame.
"Tiggy?"
My bedroom door reverberated with sounds of purring.
"Tiggy! You're alive!"
Alive and no longer in the living room, he had managed to scale the inside of the wall and make it all the way to the second floor. He had gone up instead of down.

By now, half the neighborhood was aware of the dilemma in our household, thanks to my children who had shared the story with their friends.
Around an hour later, I had half the fathers in the neighborhood assembled in my bedroom. With their tool belts slung around their expanding waistlines like so many gunslingers, they were debating how best to demolish my newly built bedroom closet.
Architect Dad, pencil poised, presented me with a diagram of my wardrobe.
"If we cut through the back of the closet wall, Pieter will be able to cover it up with ply wood."
Retired Army Dad was for blasting the wardrobe, and I was happy to see he had left his hand grenades at home.

Electrician Dad wanted to know whether there were any wires running behind the closet wall, and Plumber Dad stood by silently brandishing his snake. I have no idea what he thought he could accomplish with that tool. The cat wasn't stuck in the toilet.

After a lengthy debate, Architect Dad won and was allowed to cut the first hole into the back wall of the closet. We took turns sticking our heads through the wall, and after looking down two stories into the basement, we all came to the same conclusion.
"This is not going to work!"
The next hole went into the side of the closet but was again positioned much too high. Tiggy meowed.
"Listen!"
Everyone stopped juggling for position inside the closet.
"The cat isn't in the closet."
"No, it's underneath the floor."
"He must be sitting between the living-room ceiling and the bedroom floor."
"Pieter just laid this floor," I said, fearing the men's enthusiasm for using their power tools.
"Maybe we can cut a hole inside the closet but really close to the floor?"

Another debate ensued and everyone looked on as Army Dad put the third and final hole into the wall. We could still look down into the basement, but there was a small piece of bedroom floor sticking out under the hole like a ledge. By now it was dinner time, and wives called to retrieve their other halves. I could only imagine the conversation at dinner tables that evening.

"Did you and the other boys have fun playing with your new drill, darling?"

The other ladies in the neighborhood were probably eternally grateful that I gave their husbands the opportunity to hack, drill, and saw to their heart's content.

When the house was finally quiet again, I got on my hands and knees and crawled up to the hole near the floor.

"Tiggy!"

I stuck my arm into the hole and snaked it around until I could place my hand under the floor. It was painful because the jagged drywall dug into my skin. I waited and was rewarded with loud purring and a fuzzy cat head butting up against my hand.

"Oh, Tiggy, how are we going to get you out of here?"

I tried to grab the scruff of his neck, but he dug in his claws. He was scared, and I couldn't blame him. In order to get out, he had to twist is body one hundred eighty degrees and climb up into the closet.

I brought him food and water, which I pushed through the hole and placed on the ledge, hoping that it would keep him close. What I needed was a ramp that led from the ledge partway up the wall. Once he was on the ramp, I'd be able to grab him and lift him out without him having to twist his body.

I scoured Pieter's workshop, looking for cut-offs from his renovation projects and returned shortly with three promising ramp candidates. The first was cut too long and therefore too steep. The second went into the hole and never came back out. It fell victim to the abyss, reminding me it was a long way down to the basement.

The third and final piece of wood was perfect, but Tiggy didn't understand what he needed to do. I coaxed and called until his tiny head appeared at the rim of the ledge, but he was too frightened to set foot on my makeshift ramp.

I waited for hours with my arm dangling in the hole, ready to grab him should he emerge far enough up the ramp.

At around eleven o'clock that night, he was brave enough to climb halfway up. I grabbed hold of his fur, my arm almost too numb to pull him up, especially since he blocked the exit by clawing the ramp. It finally came loose and dangled from Tiggy's claws, preventing me from pulling him up and all the way through the hole. I held on to his scruff for dear life, and there was a tense moment when I thought I would lose him, but he tired and released the ramp. The two of them parted ways—Tiggy went up and the ramp crashed into the basement.

The next morning, I had two phone calls, the first from Pet Rescue. They had found homes for all the kittens. The second was from Pieter, checking in for a status update.

I told him:

"Dear, I've never had this much excitement before. There were four men in my bedroom, and all were after my pussy."

Whispering Spirits

Nadia, age 5:
"Grandma, when you die, you become pure energy."

As our girls grew older, it became apparent they had inherited their father's packrat gene.
We were outgrowing our three-bedroom, one-bathroom century old home we had lovingly restored over ten years. The house replacing it would have to be pretty special.
We searched for more than two years. Every time we made an offer on a house, something went wrong: our house wouldn't sell, the financing wouldn't come through in time, or someone beat us to it.

Finally, we came upon the "Old Stone House" in Craighurst, not yet officially on the market, but we were allowed an advance showing. It had been the first farmhouse in the area, built with the stones pulled from surrounding fields. Long before, the land had been severed, and now, only an acre remained around the house. The rest was fallow land.

I felt strange when I entered the house. My husband's enthusiasm was obvious as he examined every nook and cranny. By the time we reached upstairs, Pieter had mentally bought the house, but I was seized by such intense panic I couldn't leave fast enough.

"So what do you think?" he asked on our way home.
"The house doesn't want me."
I'm not sure which of us felt more surprised. I had blurted out the words before I had a chance to think.
"What?"
I tried to describe my feelings but failed miserably. He attempted to make me see reason.
"Look," he said, "if we don't go for it, that house will be gone. All country properties are going up in price, and we don't have much time. If we don't put in an offer, we'll lose it!"
I knew he was right; still . . .

We went to see the house a second time in the hope that I would feel differently. If anything, my feeling of panic grew worse the minute I went upstairs. My rational mind told me that perhaps I was simply showing signs of stress. I argued with myself that this house was a good deal, that Pieter had always wanted to own a stone house, and that living in the country had been our dream. I agreed to put in a conditional offer with the hope that it would self-destruct like all the others.
It didn't. The offer was accepted, our home sold on the first day it came on the market, and the bank approved the financing. The sequence of events was like dominos falling into place.

Once I knew that our new home was a done deal, I started announcing to friends and work colleagues that we were moving. To my surprise, it seemed that everyone knew the house.

"Did you know it's haunted?"

I was asked that question numerous times. The stories ranged from clock hands spinning in reverse to rooms with columns of air so cold you could see your breath. One person claimed to have known a previous owner who insisted that doors opened on their own and the fireplace would light itself. I called my real estate agent.

"If it's really haunted," she said, "the vendor has to state that in the disclosure form. I'll call them right away and get back to you."

She phoned again that evening.

"The house has a bit of a reputation, but "haunted" is a strong word."

We went to meet with the vendor the next weekend.

"It's not really haunted," we were assured, "more like things tend to disappear."

"Can you give me an example?" I asked.

"As a photographer, I have a dedicated drawer where I keep all my film. One day, when I went to load my camera, the drawer was empty. That struck me as odd since I always have film handy. I drove into town and bought more film. When I went to put it in my drawer, it was full again."

I decided it would be a miracle if things didn't disappear with my family around, and if that was the extent of the haunting, it wasn't too bad.

At last, the big moving day came. With the help of friends and family, we managed to move ten years of accumulated stuff. I had tried to purge as much as possible, but things I had taken out with the trash miraculously kept reappearing in the house. It would be to my benefit to move to a home with a ghost that took stuff.

Unfortunately, that wasn't how it worked. The ghost seemed to have the uncanny ability to hone in on the one item needed most at the time. The moment we moved in, the hammer disappeared.

"Where did you last see it?" I asked my husband.

"In the toolbox."

"Well, we're not buying a new one. I'm sure it'll turn up."

I wasn't going to give that ghost the satisfaction of making us buy a new hammer in the first week. It did turn up, three days later, lying on top of the toolbox.

"Pieter, did you find your hammer yet?" I called from the mudroom.

"No, it's lost or the ghost took it."

"Actually, it's right here on top of your toolbox."

He came into the mudroom to verify that the hammer was indeed lying peacefully on top of the toolbox.

"I have no idea." He shook his head and looked at me. "I took the whole thing apart looking for that hammer."

Items around the house came and went, but with a messy family like mine, I could never be certain whether it was a relative or the resident ghost that had misplaced the very thing I happened to be looking for.

For some reason, our ghost developed a liking for my bottle opener, which took a two-week vacation from the kitchen and turned up in my jewelry box. Light bulbs appeared to have a mind of their own as well, especially the ones on our dining room chandelier that blinked on and off. I began to notice this usually happened when the family was gathered around the dinner table, talking and laughing.

One evening, close to Halloween, we had a particularly lively discussion about Maya's homework project, which involved the video production of a ghost story. The chandelier began to flicker as if someone was screwing and unscrewing light bulbs.

"I think we have company," I said to the kids.

Maya, feeling particularly cocky that evening, looked up at the chandelier.

"If you know any good ghost stories, blink three times!" she said.

We all looked up expectantly.

Blink . . . blink . . . blink.

Our ghost possessed a sense of humour.

And, as I was soon to discover, it also seemed to have a

liking for music.

Whenever I sat down in the evening to play my Celtic harp, everything quieted down around me. As long as I played every evening, there were less blinking lights and missing items. If my week was busy and I too tired to play, the kids would point out that the ghost was getting restless again.

Christmas came, and so did my sister and her family. We had changed the parlour off the kitchen into a spare bedroom, and my plan was to clean the room before they arrived, but to my surprise, I found the door locked and the doorknob gone. Maybe the doorknob had come lose and fallen down. I looked around on the floor and under the kitchen table, but I knew I wouldn't find it. For some reason, the ghost had decided that the room was off limits. I broke in with a kitchen knife and began to vacuum. As I cleaned under the bed, a roll of film came sliding out.

That winter, I decided our next project would be my daughter's bedroom, which was located at the top of the back stairs leading up from the parlour. I was painting the trim when my brush slipped behind the doorframe and disappeared inside a large crack. When I pulled it out, it was covered in black soot. I stuck my hand into the crack and felt around. There was no mistake: the inside of the doorframe was completely charred.
Was this why I had felt so panic-stricken when I had first entered this room?

Had there been a fire?
Had someone died?

Our relationship with the resident ghost continued under an uneasy truce until the night I received help with dinner. I had put fresh green beans on the stove when Nadia called me from upstairs. Beans forgotten, I sat with her on her bed, looking at her artwork. Suddenly, I jumped up.

"My beans!"

I flew downstairs to the kitchen. To my amazement, I found the beans cooked to perfection and the stove turned off. Feeling a bit foolish, I looked up at the ceiling.

"Thank you! Thank you for looking after my beans."

From that moment on, something changed. I no longer felt threatened by whatever presence was in the house. I felt a connection. The ghost was a woman.

Time passed, and we soon arrived at the first anniversary of living in the old stone house. That summer, I attended my first weeklong harp workshop at the Canadian Amateur Music Centre, leaving Pieter to look after the kids and the animals. I called home to see how my husband was surviving single fatherhood.

"I don't know what's going on here," he said. "I've replaced the same light bulb in the kitchen about five times now. It's flickering like crazy."

"Maybe the ghost is missing the harp." I couldn't help teasing him.

"Whatever," he said. "Personally I think there's a short in

the wire somewhere."

He had a hard time with the whole ghost concept.

"It's not that I don't believe it," he always said. "It's just that I'm not as perceptive as you are. Besides, it scares me. It's like throwing a ball over a high wall. You don't see who's on the other side throwing it back."

When I came home after a week away, I immediately noticed that something was amiss. I felt as though a huge weight had settled on my chest as I walked in the door. It made me think of entering a smoke-filled bar after being out in the fresh night air.

Maya met me at the door. She gave me a hug then proceeded to yell at me. Surprise and confusion were written all over her face. The next moment she stopped shouting.

"Mom, I don't know why I'm yelling at you. I'm so happy you're home."

The whole family appeared tense, as if collectively perched on a giant burr, while the lights in the kitchen madly flickered on and off. Something had to be done. I started by playing the harp, which calmed things somewhat, before I resolved to call a good friend of mine.

"Loree, remember telling me that you know of a Shaman who cleanses houses? Do you still have his number?"

I called White Eagle the next day, and we booked an appointment for later that week. I made sure that everyone was out of the house that afternoon except Maya and me. We sat together and waited for him to arrive. The minutes crawled by and no car pulled into our driveway. The scene reminded me of a horror movie where the psychic was killed on the way to the exorcism. I began to fear for him.

Before allowing my fantasy to run off with me completely, I sat down at my harp and began to play. Half an hour later, White Eagle knocked on the door.
He was an elderly gentleman with long, gray hair and a kind smile. He gave me the impression that a beam of sunlight had entered my home. He introduced himself, greeting Maya and me with a hug. Then he turned to the harp.
"And here are all your spirits. They like the harp very much."
"All your sprits? You mean there is more than one?"
"Yes, there's a family here," he answered with a smile. "Let me show you."
He opened his bag and pulled from it a metal dowsing rod that he rested loosely in the palm of his hand.
"The end of the rod will point up when it encounters an energy field such as a spirit."
He walked towards the harp, and the end of the rod pointed skyward. He turned back to us.
"First, we'll light sacred herbs and smudge, cleanse ourselves, and then we will walk through the entire house, blessing each room in turn."
He reached into his bag again and produced a big drum.

"This is the heartbeat drum. Close your eyes and place your right hand over your heart."

We did as we were told, listening to the drum. A strange feeling came over me, as if the air in the room had grown thicker. Following the drum playing, he lit the smudge and instructed us to pull the smoke over our heads, down our front, back and sides three times in succession. Then he picked up his dowsing rod again and turned his attention to the spirits.

"Are you spirits of this house?"

The end of the rod went up.

"That is a yes," he said.

"Have you experienced pain in this place?"

The rod again signaled yes.

"Please show us."

The tip of the rod pointed us towards the kitchen. We walked through into the parlour and up the back stairs. I had a pretty good idea where we were headed, but decided to wait and see. Following White Eagle and his dowsing rod upstairs, we moved towards my daughter's room.

In the doorway, the dowsing rod swung wildly from side to side, and he stopped.

"This is like a portal. There is something here," he said.

I showed him the crack in the doorframe and instructed him to stick his hand inside. Moments later he looked at his charcoal covered hand.

"Fire," he said, and turned his attention back to the spirits.

"What do you like about this room?" he asked.

The dowsing rod led him from one window to the other.

"The spirits are children of the light," he said. "We could ask them to leave, but it would be a shame. We can just remove the energy of their pain. They belong to this house, and they are your spirit guides. They will help to protect you. See, they are standing beside you."

He directed his rod to my left side and it pointed up. Then he aimed it at Maya's right side, and again, the rod pointed up.

We made our way through the entire house, cleansing and blessing each room. Arriving back in the living room, he asked me to play the harp for him, and I was happy to do so.

"There are three spirits in your house, a mother, father, and a young child. You will get to know each of them and will be able to tell them apart."

We ended his visit with refreshments, and he left before Pieter and the other girls returned home.

That night I dreamt of a young woman with shoulder-length, dark hair. She wore a long, washed-out, lilac-colored dress. Her face looked kind but serious and sad. I awoke to her words.

"Everything is all right, now that Victoria is here!"

Startled, I sat up in bed. The room was dark—no one was there. As I became more alert, I noticed a beautiful floral scent. I felt scared to death and excited at the same time. Hesitantly, I whispered into the dark.

"Are you of the light?"

In answer, the room was filled with the smell of flowers. I knew it meant yes. Now wide awake, I sat up in bed, aware that my nose was completely stuffed with seasonal allergies. There was no way I should have been able to smell anything. As soon as I began to think rationally, the scent disappeared. I lay back down and waited, but nothing more happened that night.

The next night, I had my second visitor. I awoke to a child's voice whispering baby talk in my left ear. I couldn't understand a word but knew I hadn't dreamt it.

On the third night, as I drifted off to sleep, I became aware of a male presence close to me. Again, there was a scent associated with the visit, but it wasn't very strong and reminded me a little of garlic. It was enough, however, to make me sit up and look around the room. One thing was certain: the spirits were trying to make contact.

The next afternoon, Pieter and I were about to sit down with a cup of coffee. I had just brewed a fresh pot and the smell permeated the house. We stood not a foot apart when I felt almost overwhelmed by the same floral scent that had awoken me a few nights before. This time the smell was accompanied by an overpowering emotion of joy. Something inside me responded. It felt as if my soul were attempting to escape from my body and drift upwards into this joy. Victoria had given me a glimpse of heaven. It was her thank-you to me. I felt this message very strongly. Within that second, my soul connected with the other side, and a shift took place inside me. All my fears left me.

I turned to my husband.

"Pieter, can you smell it? Can you feel it? It's all around us!"

"I smell coffee."

As soon as I had tried to share the experience, both the feeling and the scent disappeared as quickly as it had come. The message had been meant for me alone.

We lived for another eight years in the old stone house without any further contact from our spirits. However, after we moved out, the new owners called me within three days and reported doors banging shut, knocking on windows, and columns of cold air.

The spirits obviously didn't like the house changing owners. I gave them White Eagle's phone number, wondering what the house had in store for them.

What message might the spirits have for the new owners?

Stink and Think

When we thought the children were old enough to have a family dog, my husband, Pieter, and I ventured to the local library to do some research. (That's what was done in the olden days before the Internet.). We found a big book on breeds and started to leaf through. I had grown up around my uncle's Great Danes, and Pieter had owned a German Shepherd as a boy, so both of us favored large-breed dogs.

Midway through the book, I found a page that made my heart skip a beat. It featured a mountain range, and majestically poised on top were three gigantic, long-haired dogs. The page was entitled "Leonberger – the European Babysitter."

The breed originated in Germany, where the dog-loving mayor of the town of Leonberg (Lion Mountain) had created a mixed breed using Newfoundland, St. Bernard, and Great Pyrenees. He succeeded in creating a town mascot that resembled a lion in stature.

When we had finished reading about the breed, both Pieter and I were sold. This was the dog for us! Unfortunately, there were no Leonbergers in Canada at the time, so I began the search in my home country of Germany. One year later, Gandolf, Lion of Walhall, was flown to Canada to become our first family dog.

Shortly after moving to the country, he made the acquaintance of a skunk.

I had let him out for his morning communion with nature, and fearing no evil, I opened the door when he whined to be let in. He charged into the house, lovingly brushing up against my robe and hands. By the time I got the first whiff, it was already too late. He went back outside faster than he had come in, undoubtedly feeling highly mistreated. I raced to the downstairs bathroom but found the door had been locked by Pieter, who was in the shower. In response to my insistent knocking, he opened the door and curled his nose.

"Why do I smell skunk?"

I went upstairs to wake the kids.

The youngest yelled at me. "Don't turn on the light, it's too bright!"

The oldest yelled in a similar vein. "Mommy, turn on the light, or I'll go back to sleep!"

The middle one didn't yell at all but simply slept on. If a cannon had exploded beside her head, I'm not sure she would have heard it. I rubbed her back, shook her by the shoulders, and tousled her hair until she was awake enough to mumble something vaguely coherent.

"Okay, okay. I'm up already. Mom, why do you smell like skunk?"

Downstairs, Pieter made the rounds with a Febreze bottle, spraying anything that smelled suspicious. I got a full dose down the front of my robe, leaving it clinging wet and cold against my skin.

We now ran behind schedule and were late for school—again. I rushed into the upstairs bathroom to help Nadia with her hair.

"Mom? Why was the earth made?" she asked.

I paused before deciding on my answer. "Because God wanted to."

She didn't miss a beat. "And who decided to make God?"

Before I had a chance to think, she asked: "How did God make Jesus?"

My mind raced through all the possible answers I could give a six year old.

Then she said: "I know how he did it! God is both male and female. That's how he did it."

Lucia came into the bathroom, which was becoming decidedly crowded.

"Mom, are we poor?"

"No, you couldn't say that."

"Would you then classify us as middle-class aristocrats?"

It took me a while to consider this since my mind was still preoccupied by who might have made God.

Maya, bless her young soul, was not in a reflective mood that morning and got me off the hook by yelling at the entire assembly.

"Will you guys shut up and hurry up! We're really late this morning! Mom, what am I going to tell my teacher?"

Yeah, what indeed?

"Well," I said slowly, "I think you can blame this morning on reeking Rover and an overdose of philosophy."

The Untold Tale

In the spring of Gandolf's tenth year, I noticed that he had begun to limp. Assuming that he simply had sprained his front leg, Pieter and I took him to our vet of twenty-five years. Dr. Fisher examined the lump on Gandolf's leg and ordered an x-ray. He looked grim while he explained that Gandolf had bone cancer.
"You still have time," he said. "You don't need to make a decision right away."

I left the vet's office in a daze. From that moment on, my entire life revolved around one question: "When is the right time to let him go?"
Until then, I had never been faced with having to make this decision for one of my pets. They had all left me suddenly and unexpectedly. This was a different kind of loss. I didn't know what to expect.

"He will tell you when it's the right time," a friend told me.
She had lost her dog to cancer a couple of years before.

I waited and watched for a sign from Gandolf—something that would tell me it was time. There was nothing I could sense from him. The lump continued to grow at an alarming rate, and my once-so-youthful friend slowed more and more.

Spring turned into summer, and I felt time slipping away. Every day my fear grew that Gandolf would collapse outside and be unable to climb the few steps into the house. He weighed one hundred fifty pounds. What if something happened while Pieter and I were at work and our girls where home alone with him?

By August it became clear to me that time was about to run out. I tried to involve Pieter in the decision since he had told me that his parents had not given him the chance to say good-bye to his beloved Shepherd, Kurt. But every time I broached the subject, he found a way to derail the conversation.

There came the day when he planned to take the girls to Toronto for an evening performance of Shakespeare in the Park. I knew they wouldn't be back before midnight, and I made my decision. That morning, before they left, I asked Pieter to come outside and help me pick Gandolf's final resting place. He reluctantly followed me to the deck where Gandolf stood watching me walk around the yard. I picked the back corner under a young birch tree, and Pieter agreed it was good spot.
"He'll be able to overlook the entire yard and house from there," he said, his voice cracking.

As soon as the family left, I picked up the phone and called Dr. Fisher. I explained the situation, and he agreed to come to our place in the afternoon.

I began to dig. The day was sweltering hot. I dug and cried and dug some more until I was exhausted. Then I went inside and lay down beside Gandolf on the living-room floor as we had done so many times before. As I lay there, snuggled up to his back, I let the memories of our lifetime together run through my mind.

I had flown to Germany with Gail, a breeder who wanted to add a Leonberger to her kennel. Equipped with a Eurail pass and a breeder's list, we travelled through Germany for two weeks, visiting every breeder who agreed to see us.

We ended up staying a night at a castle owned by Prince Von Rotenau and his mother, the Princess Von Rotenau. When we went out to dinner with them, everyone in the small village addressed them by their title and bowed or curtsied.

The castle was more of a fortress than a Disney palace, but it did have a large ballroom that was completely empty except for a small plastic card table at which the princess served us a roasted goose at midnight. The hallways had twelve-foot high ceilings and were adorned with huge oak wardrobes that towered over us. Looking up, I spotted the princess's parrot sharpening his beak on the antique giants. The castle moat served as the kennel for ten Leonbergers that roamed the moat on guard duty at night, while the ballroom doubled as a gym for the princess's French bulldogs. Before we left, my travel companion, Gail, purchased a female Leonberger from the prince.

With only one day to go, we still hadn't found a male for me. There was one last visit to make in the north of Germany. A litter had just been born. I picked Gandolf when he was one day old, nothing more than a handful.

He flew to Canada at the age of eight weeks. Gail and I drove to the airport and picked him up the week after Christmas. He was rambunctious and knocked the kids flying, chewed the legs of our kitchen table, and was the holy terror of the puppy kindergarten class.

When he was two years old, I bought him a harness, and we joined 'The Good Guys,' a group of dedicated dog owners and their canine companions who gave cart-and-sleigh-rides to raise money for Canine Vision and kids' cancer camps.
Gandolf soon became a favourite of the group.
He often gave our girls a ride to or from school in the wagon or the toboggan, and he tirelessly followed the kids around the yard, watching over them.

Just how protective he was of our children became clear when my sister visited with us and played catch with the girls. She had just caught a screaming Lucia when Gandolf came from behind and jumped up. There was no growl or other hostile behaviour. He simply stood on his hind legs and held her in place with his paws on her shoulders. As soon as she released Lucia, he jumped down and trotted off as if nothing had happened.

My mind returned to the present, and I buried my face in his fur and wept. He was very perceptive, and when I realized that my tears worried him, I went back outside and dug some more.

Dr. Fisher arrived at 3:00 p.m., and we let Gandolf out for a final walk. The vet watched thoughtfully as Gandolf limped over to one of the apple trees.
"You know, if he was mine, I think I would do the same thing."
Having Dr. Fisher's blessing that I was making the right decision meant the world to me. Perhaps he knew it. We went back inside, and Gandolf enjoyed a large piece of Salami on the living room carpet.

"The family doesn't know you're here," I said. "I want them to think that Gandolf went on his own."
"I understand. I won't shave his paw, and nobody needs to know I was here."

I sat down beside my furry friend. He looked up at me with a questioning gaze while Dr. Fisher gave him a sedative. Gandolf kept his eyes on me until his head became too heavy to hold up, and he laid it down in my lap.

Dr. Fisher waited for him to go to sleep before performing euthanasia.

I don't know how long I lay on the living room floor after Dr. Fisher left. When the pain of my loss and the enormity of my decision became too much, I went back outside and dug some more. I shovelled dirt and rocks until the sun went down.

Exhausted physically and emotionally, I went inside and lay down on the sofa in the living room, Gandolf by my feet, waiting for the family to return.

At one o'clock in the morning, I heard a car pull up to the house and the doors slam. I sat up. The front door opened and the girls walked in, Maya in the lead.

"Oh, Mom, you're still up?" Her eyes fell on Gandolf, who had never before failed to greet her by the door.

"How is Gandolf?" I heard the uncertainty in her voice.

Slowly the girls came into the living room.

"Is he…?" Lucia couldn't finish the sentence. I nodded.

"He fell asleep peacefully this afternoon. Just as we were all hoping he would."

We got his blanket, and wrapping it around him, we gently carried him outside.

After the girls had gone to bed, I turned to Pieter to tell him the truth, but before I could get started, he cut me off.

"I'm so glad Gandolf picked his own time, and we didn't have to make a decision."

The next morning, we placed all of Gandolf's belongings into his grave: his harness, his bowls, his favourite ball, and his collar. Then we carefully lowered him, and the girls covered him in flowers until he was no longer visible. Pieter filled the grave with dirt and placed a big fieldstone at the head.

Over the next few weeks, I made a number of attempts to let Pieter in on my white lie, but he always forestalled me.
"I'm so glad Gandolf made his own decision."
Finally, I gave up.

Puppy Obedience

After we lost our beautiful canine companion, Gandolf, I contacted the breeder in Germany and asked if she had continued to breed with Gandolf's line.

"Yes," she said. "As a matter of fact, I have his great-nephew, Dumbledore, available. He was just born yesterday."

In November of 2003, Dumbledore joined our family.

At four months old, we started puppy obedience training. For the first class, we were to leave our dogs at home so that we could discuss class etiquette and our homework for the next week. This was demonstrated using a German Shepard puppy that obliged his trainer almost immediately.

With renewed hope and enthusiasm, I went home ready to try our first exercise: the Settle. Put dog on leash, stand on leash, ignore dog, no eye contact. Dog will settle down. Release dog after twenty minutes. How hard could it be? The Shepard lay down within the first five minutes.

I gave Dumbledore a few minutes to calm down before starting the exercise, but my first obstacle was the fact that he had no collar on at the time.

This is what my Settle exercise looked like with a sixty-five pound Leonberger puppy:

Catch dog by scruff of neck and offer treat while attaching collar. Avoid paws in face while dog wriggles around on his back. Avoid teeth in hand while dog clamps jaws around wrist. Attach leash. I am now ready to stand on leash.

For this exercise, I suggest heavy, steel-toed boots and shin guards as dog will bite ankles and legs in frustration. Do not dance on leash but try to endure pain quietly and ignore dog as he clamps jaws firmly around your calves. As soon as dog takes a second's rest, release him from the Settle and pretend the exercise has been a success. Snap leash off collar and stop bleeding by applying pressure to gash in arm. Investigate wound to see if stitches are needed. Get family member with nursing background to apply bandage with antiseptic to arm.

I'm happy to say that both Dumbledore and I survived puppy obedience classes and were awarded the dubious distinction of "Best Improved Dog."

The Hilton Hotel

Dumbledore grew to become a magnificent representative of his breed and soon caught the eye of breeders all over Canada as well as the United States. I let them convince me to spend hundreds of dollars on his breeding clearances with the promise that he would earn this money back with just one breeding. I was further assured, as the owner of the sire, that I hardly had any work. I naively pictured sitting in the comfort of my living room having coffee and cake with various breeders while waiting for Mother Nature to take its course in my backyard.

Late one Monday evening, I received a phone call from a breeder in Quebec. Pauline and I chatted for an hour, and she told me she would like Dumbledore to be the father of Florence's litter. Florence was in heat and her progesterone was going up daily. She would most likely be ready by the weekend.

"Great," I thought. "I'll get my spare room ready for Pauline and Florence, and we'll have a nice visit."

But Pauline had hoped for chilled semen, because the thought of a thirteen-hour drive didn't appeal to her. I told her that I didn't have the foggiest idea when it came to dog breeding.

"Not to worry. I will talk you through it. The first thing

you have to do is empty your dog."
"Really? And how do I do that?" I asked.
"Ask your husband to do to the dog what every young man does to himself."
I could only imagine Pieter's reaction coming home from a twelve-hour shift at the hospital and have his wife ask him to "do the dog."
As expected, he said: "You want me to do what?"
He eyed the dog all evening with great apprehension.

The next day, I spoke to a fertility vet about collecting chilled semen.
"First, you need to order a chilled-semen kit from Winnipeg. Then you have to bring in both Dumbledore and a female in heat. It doesn't have to be another Leonberger—any breed will do. Three days before the collection, you'll have to empty your dog, so today or tomorrow will be fine".

I hung up the phone. Where was I going to find a female in heat? They weren't exactly a dime a dozen. This was a lot more information than I ever wanted to know about dog breeding.

That evening, I made Pieter an especially nice dinner with a glass of wine to relax him before I broached the subject of "emptying the dog" again. I guess he realized he couldn't evade my request much longer.
"You owe me big time!" he said, looking at me balefully as

he and Dumbledore went off to the back room accompanied by howls of "Uughh—gross!" from our three daughters.
I followed reluctantly. There was Pieter on his knees, trying to figure out how to touch Dumbledore in the least offensive manner possible. Dumbly released one growl, and we gave up.

I emailed Pauline the bad news, but she was not discouraged. She had a plan, which involved sending me a bloody towel infused with Florence's scent via Purolator. She had also talked to her vet, Dr. Stahl, who was attending a reproduction conference at the Airport Hilton Hotel. If I were willing to drive Dumbledore and the scent-infused towel to Toronto, Dr. Stahl agreed to collect him during her lunch hour and fly the semen back to Montreal.

Pauline's package arrived the very next day, but nobody was home to sign for it. That evening, I drove across town to pick up and sign for a bloody towel. My kids were convinced I had a screw loose, and Pieter was likely in agreement. Did I mention that he's now scarred for life?

When I came home with my towel, the family was close to starvation. I threw some hamburgers onto the barbecue before turning my attention to the problem at hand. While my burgers did their thing on the barbie, I unpacked Dumbledore's treasure. Making a big deal of it,

I tried to get him excited about his package. After all, how many dogs get a mail-order bride?

He sniffed and sniffed and then turned his attention to the barbecue. The towel lay forgotten while Dumbledore stalked the hamburgers. I tried again later that night and early the next morning, but he wasn't interested. I started to have my doubts that Dumbledore would ever become a dad. How was Dr. Stahl going to convince him to make a donation? Did the Hilton allow dogs? I imagined walking into the front lobby with a dog the size of a small horse weighing some one hundred fifty pounds and looking like a bear. Were we going to "do it" in the front foyer of the Hilton?

That evening, I spoke to Dr. Stahl on the phone. She didn't sound much more confident than I did. She had never done "it" in a hotel either, but was willing to try. That made two of us. She also told me not to worry about emptying the dog, which made Pieter very happy.

The following morning, after a sleepless night, we were off to the big city with our stud in tow. Dr. Stahl met us at Reception, and Dumbledore made the acquaintance of marble floors, mirrors, sliding doors, and elevators. Luckily, like a true Leo, Dumbly turned out to be an emotional athlete, taking all these new things in stride. Dr. Stahl had to sign a waiver, and we were allowed up to her room. She retrieved her chilled semen kit from the hotel fridge, laughing that the hotel had no idea what they were keeping cool in there.

I had brought a big bed sheet, which we spread over the floor, and we were ready to begin. Obviously, all Dumbledore needed was a woman's touch, and Dr Stahl's was pure magic. She convinced Dumbledore to give her not just one, but two, donations. He left the hotel crossed-eyed, not quite walking straight, and with a silly grin on his furry face.

The semen reached Montreal by nine thirty that evening, and Dr. Stahl determined that it had good concentration and motility. After some initial objection from Florence, she was bred that evening and again the next morning.

Eight weeks later, Pauline called.

"Congratulations! Dumbledore is a Daddy. We have eleven puppies!"

By the end of the following year, Dumbledore had fathered another nineteen puppies. We rewarded him with a wife of his very own.

Kaia, Lion of Walhall, joined our family in the spring of 2007.

The Mouse Days of Winter

If there is such a thing as the dog days of summer, then there should also be the mouse days of winter. Living in a drafty, century home in the country definitely had its drawbacks. There were plenty of opportunities for mice, and even chipmunks, to come in and make a cozy nest for the winter. As soon as the thermometer dropped to single digits, we had an influx of rodents. It was like a mouse convention in my kitchen pantry. After pulling out several empty boxes of cereal and crackers, now filled primarily with droppings, I declared war on my pantry raiders.

This resolution was short lived. It took only a few mornings of pulling limp little bodies and one amputee from my cupboard before my heart softened. There had to be a better way.

I discussed the problem with a neighbor in the mousetrap section of the local hardware store. His solution was to live-trap the critters and let them wait out the winter in a metal garbage can. In the spring, he intended to drive them to a nearby forest and give them freedom.

This seemed like a perfectly good idea. I bought a live-trap and a metal garbage can. Our mudroom was the perfect spot for my mouse condominium as it already housed Lucia's bunny, Maya's ferret, and Kaia, our second Leonberger. Adding sawdust bedding to complete the setup, I stepped back to admire my handiwork.

The next morning, I approached the pantry full of anticipation, but my enthusiasm was short-lived. The trap was empty. It took a few more nightly attempts of loading it with various tantalizing bait before I had my first garbage-can resident. Once the trap was broken in, it attracted one mouse per night and sometimes two. As I added newcomers to the mouse hotel, I noticed that the inhabitants were shivering, so I dug up a couple of outgrown mittens and a scarf that I donated to the mice for warmth. Soon, the garbage can was teeming with residents. I lost count after twenty.

One morning, a month after the inception of the hotel, I awoke to something brushing up against the back of my head. I reached back and my hand made contact with a mouse. I jumped up, scaring my cat, Meeko, cuddled up next to me fast asleep.
"Some cat you are!" I said as he eyed me reproachfully.
With the mouse gone, I lay back down, wondering if it had been an escapee from the hotel or a prospective new resident. After a few minutes, I had almost drifted back to sleep, I felt something move across my pillow. The mouse was back, trying to nest in my hair. I made grab for it, but it escaped, running over my pillow and past Meeko's nose.

I lay down again, straining my ears for the sound of little feet. All was quiet.

Just as I dozed off, Nadia sounded the alarm.
"Mom! There's a mouse in my bed!"
This time, it was Pieter who came to the rescue. The mouse had switched beds and now sat on top of Nadia's blanket. Pieter managed to catch it and put it in a class jar. On closer inspection, I felt sure the mouse was not long for this world. However, it recovered quickly with the help of a piece of cheese, and it occurred to me this was a rather fat mouse that had figured my braid would make a good nest, and I, a good midwife.

Before I had a chance to go back to bed, Kaia began her morning serenade with the beautiful soprano voice she used to its full potential. I shuffled downstairs to be greeted by Dumbledore, who gave me a long-suffering look that clearly said he agreed with me: it was indeed much too early to be up. I followed the dogs through the mudroom to the back door, and there, rolling around on its side, was my mouse hotel.
"Kaia!"

Once the dogs were in the yard and my mostly empty can upright again, I made my way to the bathroom. I closed the door and turned towards the toilet. There, clinging to the side of the bowl, was another mouse. It had just finished doing laps and had trouble exiting the swimming pool. It looked up at me, eyes wide with fear, trying to deduce what was coming. I stared back, thoughts racing. How was I going to capture a bathing mouse? Gloves! I ran to the front door, but among the several sets, all I could find were left-handed gloves. I began to regret my generous donation of mittens.

Oven mitts! I owned a pair that recently had suffered third-degree burns. I ran into the kitchen, grabbed the charred mitts, and approached the toilet with caution.
The mouse looked up wearily, sensing that I had plans. I attempted to place one mitt under the mouse, but it clearly interpreted this as a hostile action and jumped, landing with a splash, back into the water. It crossed the bowl in record time, and then tried to ascend on the other side, my mittened hand in hot pursuit. I lifted the mouse slightly, and this time it managed to jump out and onto the toilet plunger, climbing nimbly down the wooden handle. I sat down on the toilet. What a morning!

Snoopy, our other cat, came slinking into the bathroom showing a great deal of interest in the toilet. Aha! So that's how the mouse had got in there. Meanwhile, Dumbledore had opened the back door and Kaia careened into the stamp-sized bathroom in an attempt to corner Snoopy. This was a favorite past time. She was closely followed by Dumbledore, who immediately recognized his opportunity and pressed his advantage. While Kaia's front end was preoccupied and wedged between the toilet and the shower, Dumbledore squeezed into the bathroom, his intentions obviously not those of a gentleman. I remained pinned to the toilet by my food chain.

I wonder what went through Pieter's mind as he appeared sleepily in the doorway. I don't think he noticed the little brown blur that ran through his legs and out the door.

The Perfect Christmas Tree

"How about we get a real tree this year instead of using the old fake one again?"

My husband, Pieter, stood in the family room of our new country home looking up at the cathedral ceiling. The angle of his tilted head made me wonder about the size of tree he visualized in his mind's eye.

The next weekend he talked me into bundling up our three daughters, and we embarked in the aging van on what was to become The Great Christmas-Tree Hunt. It was a cloudy but pleasantly warm day as we drove, carolling through the snow-covered countryside. We pulled up to the Christmas-tree farm and discovered that a warm winter's day was not necessarily an advantage to finding the perfect tree. The parking lot was a muddy mess and so was our van by the time we had parked. We sloshed over to the horse-drawn sleigh.

"This is not a sleigh—it's a wagon!" Maya, our oldest, sounded indignant.

The driver smiled and explained there was just not enough snow on the mucky path for the horses to pull a sleigh. She was mollified and climbed up, but Nadia, our youngest, looked around and noticed that her father was the only one without an axe or saw.

"How are you going to chop down the tree, Daddy?"

I looked at my husband's sheepish smile. "I think Daddy is intending to pull it up by the roots."

We let the horses take us deep into the forest before we climbed off and set out into the trees. The tinkling sound of the horses' bells had not yet faded away when we came to an abrupt halt. Nadia had the habit of running ahead, and she had disappeared into a giant snowdrift. There was enough snow off the path to make us sink beyond our knees. We dug her out and began darting among the trees, tossing snow at each other and making sure our upper bodies were as drenched as our legs.

We had yet to decide which tree would grace our family room for the season. Lucia offered the first suggestion.

"This one looks sad," she said, pointing at a scraggly tree with a crooked top. "We should pick it."

She always had a soft spot for the underdog. Not so Maya, who complained loudly that she didn't want an ugly tree in the house. While the two older kids heatedly debated the potential tree candidate, the smallest of the lot picked the largest specimen she could find. My husband did his best to tune out the kids and commune with nature while keeping an eye out for a fellow tree seeker who might be equipped with an axe.

As soon as he spotted another male brandishing a big

yellow saw, he beckoned all of us to follow and picked the next best tree in the vicinity of the saw bearer. Now that the excitement had worn off, everyone became aware of cold, wet feet. The horse wagon could not come soon enough. We hopped on and looked expectantly at Dad to follow with our prized possession that he dragged, huffing and puffing, through the snow. He stood hesitantly at the back of the wagon, obviously stumped by the problem of how to hoist the twelve-foot tree.

"C'mon, Dad!" our youngest hollered encouragingly.

But Dad waved us on with a resigned expression that revealed his eagerness to make the journey on foot. He had no choice. The tree just didn't fit.

We waited for him at the checkout point where, to our relief, a fire blazed, warming our numb limbs and melting the soles of my daughters' boots.

By now it was late in the afternoon, and the Christmas-tree farm was preparing to close. I left the kids by the fire and under the watchful eye of the proprietor while I went to get the van. It was the only vehicle in the muddy lot and I reflected on how sad it looked covered in dirt, rust, and dents. As I made my way across the puddle-ridden surface, I noticed that the slushy ground was slightly frozen. The temperature had dropped considerably and the sky looked rather ominous. It was high time to head home.

As I opened the car door, I stepped into a greenish-yellow

puddle. This meant nothing to me other than more wet feet. I climbed in and drove up to the gate where my husband finally appeared. He looked tired and waved an arm that seemed longer than the other. His enthusiasm for a real tree had been greatly dampened.

We paid for our oversized shrub and for once didn't have to wait for the kids to fight over the seating arrangement in the van. Wet and tired, they climbed in without much fuss.
"Okay, you take the top, and I'll take the trunk." Pieter said.
I looked at him with my best you've-got-to-be-kidding expression. The van was taller than I was. How could he expect me to be of any help manhandling the tree on top? I was likely to end up hanging from the "roofed" tree when we were finished.
Somehow we managed it, with my husband putting real muscle into the effort and me pretending to do the same.

Then we were off, our spirits slowly restored by the expectation of returning home to hot chocolate and cookies by the fire.
"Dear, I believe there's smoke coming from under the hood."
I glanced over at the temperature gage, and an unprintable word escaped my lips. The indicator was past "H" and off the scale. We stopped by the side of the road and looked at each other.

Now what?

He got out and approached the hood as carefully as a thief would a prized jewel.

"Be careful!" I yelled, unnecessarily, since Pieter appeared uncomfortable enough with the idea of opening the hood. He determined in short order that we were out of cooling fluid. A thought dawned on me.

"Uh . . . Dear, what does cooling fluid look like?"

"Sort of yellowish-green. Why?"

"Oh, nothing. I just stepped into a large puddle of it in the parking lot."

He did a classic double take while I gave him a stupid grin.

"Mom, is the car broken?" asked Lucia.

I sighed. "Yes, I think so, Dear."

Thank God for modern technology and cell phones. After a quick discussion about which of our friends would be privileged with the task of rescuing us, we made a few calls until we found the perfect candidates: a young couple with van and no children. We waited as the sky around us grew darker and the windshield filled with large fluffy flakes. Without heat in the car, our wet fingers and toes became numb while our spirits fell along with the temperature.

The cavalry arrived and transferred our frozen family into their warm vehicle. We watched as the two men hummed and hawed over our van, alternately pouring in cooling fluid then crawling underneath to see where it would squirt out. After several unsuccessful attempts to get the van moving, it was decided to simply take us home and have the van towed.

It was almost dark, and snow swirled around us, severely limiting visibility. Flash freezing had made the roads treacherous, and on more than one occasion, I thought we would end up in the ditch before the day was done.
"What about our tree?" Nadia asked worriedly.
"Who cares!" said Maya.
By the time we arrived home, it was completely dark outside and our driveway barely visible in the swirling snow.

After thanking our friends and wishing them a safe trip home, I unlocked the front door.
"Mom, what's this?" Maya held up a piece of paper she had picked up from under the door.
I took it from her and read the notice. "A load-limiting device has been installed on your electrical panel. If you do not settle your account within 3 days, your power will be shut off entirely. Please call . . ."
"What does that mean?" Lucia asked.
We found out pretty quickly what it meant: I could turn on a light while the furnace ran, but when I tried to put a pot of soup on the stove, I had exceeded the allotted amount of electricity. The house went pitch black. I stepped outside, flipped the breaker, and filled my slippers with snow.

Meanwhile, Pieter tried to persuade any tow truck operator he could reach to head out into the storm and rescue the van. He had all but exhausted the selection from the yellow pages.

"They're either out, or they don't want to go out in weather like this," he said.

He got lucky on his final attempt and made arrangements to meet the tow truck by the van in one hour. I was worried and didn't want him to leave.

"I have to go. The tree is still on top of the van."

I was sure he was cursing the day he had decided on a real tree when all he had to do was descend the basement steps to retrieve the fake one.

Pieter changed into dry clothes and headed out into the storm, armed with a few yards of rope. I spent the evening alternating between overloading the newly installed electrical breaker and shaking snow out of my slippers.

As it turned out, the electrical company had been sending the bills to the wrong address. Since I was new to country living and had been advised that the meter was estimated monthly and read quarterly, I had assumed that bills were also sent out quarterly rather than monthly. It appeared that the electrical company could only find the correct address to install a load-limiting device and leave a threatening note.

The kids went to bed and the hours trickled by. I worried

about my husband out in the raging blizzard, not daring to turn on the TV to pass the time lest I overload the confounded device outside. I felt relieved to hear a car drive up the lane, and the next minute Pieter stepped through the door, looking like the abominable snowman. Tired and covered in dirt and snow, he described his adventure.

"I arrived about half an hour before the tow truck. So I decided to move the tree from the van to the car."

"By yourself?" I asked, interrupting.

"Well, yes. I managed to get it off the van and onto the car, but then I realized my rope was still on the front seat. I bent down to get it, and when I stood up, the tree was gone."

"Gone?" Where did it go?"

"The wind took it and blew it across the street."

"Oh no —what did you do?"

"I chased it down the road and caught it just before it headed into the opposite ditch."

We looked at each other and started to laugh. The mental image of Pieter chasing our Christmas tree down Highway 93 was just too funny.

"Where is it now?" I asked.

"Lying in the driveway," he said with a tired voice. "I'm going to bed."

By the next morning, the sun shone brightly, and we looked out the window with renewed spirits. There was no driveway, no car and no Christmas tree. Instead, there was a three-foot high snowdrift in front of the door. I took my chances with overloading the electricity and turned on the radio, which announced that stores were closed, buses cancelled, and people were stranded all over the place. Naturally, the electrical company was not about to send out one of their employees to remove the device, even if they had received their money via telephone banking by now.

Armed with a snow blower and shovels, the family headed out to find the Christmas tree for a second time in as many days. After hours of digging, we managed to tunnel up the lane to the road, just ahead of the snowplough whose driver waved at us cheerfully as he barricaded our driveway. We continued to dig and finally unearthed the car as well as the tree, which we stood up and leaned against a large snowdrift. It was caked with ice and snow.

"We better leave it outside and let some of this stuff drop off," Pieter said.

For another few days, we left it outside, where it got snowed on daily.

With Christmas around the corner, we had no choice but to bring it into the house. We pulled and pushed. With extra layers of ice and snow, it now weighed twice as much as before.

"Into the mudroom!" I grunted with the effort of lifting the tree through the door.

It almost fit. Every time I walked from the kitchen to the

dining room, I had to climb over the trunk that extended well beyond the doorway.

The ice and snow on the tree began to melt. By the next day, the mudroom and part of the kitchen were under water. We waited a couple of days until the worst of the flood had subsided before we decided it was time to place the tree in its proper spot. We moved all the furniture against the wall and heaved it into the family room where Pieter secured its tip to a ceiling beam.
"It needs water," he said, looking at the dripping tree.
Before I could think of a clever retort, I noticed that both the cat and the dog were studying the newly erected foliage with great interest.
"Don't you guys even think about it! There will be no climbing or leg lifting inside the house."

Everyone crowded around. Indoors and without competition from its peers, it looked even larger than it had in the forest. The kids danced around the enormous tree, delighted by the fact that even with outstretched arms and on tiptoes, they could only reach up to its middle.
"It's big, isn't it?" Pieter said, looking up with adoration and pride.
"Yuck! My feet are all wet!" Nadia held up her foot with an accusing expression.
Maya laughed. "It's green!"
Everyone picked up their feet and looked at their once more-or-less white socks, all of which had turned the color

of the family room carpet.

"The tree is melting the carpet!" Nadia yelled. Whenever she got excited, the volume of her voice rose a few decibels.

"Mom," Lucia said with a meaningful look, "Santa better wrap all his presents in green paper this year before he puts them under the tree."

I sent the kids to bed and covered the floor with old sheets while my husband retrieved box after box of ornaments and lights from the basement. Tree decorating was a job he shared with no one. It allowed him to unfold his artistic flair to its fullest. He whistled Christmas carols and placed decorations all over the tree, while I went into the dining room, lit a candle, and begun to wrap presents.

His whistling stopped suddenly.

"Dear, could you come here for a minute?"

I left my partially wrapped book and went into the family room. Peter studied his handiwork with a sheepish expression. He had run out of lights after covering only the bottom three feet of the tree. Not only was it taller than its synthetic brother, it was also almost three times as big around.

"I guess you need more lights."

I shrugged my shoulders in resignation and headed back to the dining room with Pieter trailing after me. Having the dubious pleasure of being the family's finance minister, I was not in good spirits these days. The van repair and the hydro bill had severely depleted our funds. The last thing I wanted to do was spend money on Christmas-tree lights.

We entered the dining room and the sight that met my eyes chased all financial worries from my mind. The candle had burnt down to its decorative wreath, which had melted, setting the tablecloth and book with wrapping paper on fire. We stood rooted to the floor for a moment.
"Fire!" I screamed, as if that was going to help. Luckily, Pieter was faster on the uptake. He grabbed the edge of the tablecloth and smothered the flames. I stood in shock as little bits of charcoaled wrapping paper settled in my hair.
"My tablecloth," was all I could say.
Pieter surveyed the charred book. "You're lucky you didn't lose more than that," he said. "Whose present was that?"
"Yours."
"That figures." He smiled and gave me a hug. I must have looked like I really needed it.

When Christmas finally came, the carpet was dry again, the van repaired, the electricity on, the fire out, the tree decorated, and the bank account in overdraft. We all stood under our massive tree and marvelled at the lights high above our heads.
Grandma broke the silence.
"When you're a child, the Christmas tree is always taller than you are, but when you grow up, you lose that magical feeling when the tree towers over you."
She paused, searching for the right words.
"This is the first time, since my childhood, that standing

under a Christmas tree, I feel the magic of Christmas like I used to."

My husband and I looked at each other over the upturned and smiling faces of our children and parents.

"I guess it was worth it. Want to do it again next year?"

Grand Bahama Island

Travelling with my sister, Jaqui, was always an adventure. She was the spur-of-the-moment type while I planned everything to the last detail. She usually sprung these surprise trips on me as an impromptu birthday present. It always started the same way: "I found this really cheap deal." One of her bargain-basement trips led to a mid-winter visit to Venice where the temperature was so icy, we both returned with a cold. On another occasion, we ended up in a converted monastery on Margarita Island where we were awoken at the crack of dawn by the roosters housed in the backyard.

When my phone rang late one January evening just before my birthday, and I heard, "I found us a really cheap trip!" I met her announcement with carefully guarded enthusiasm.
"Where are we going?" I asked.
"Grand Bahama Island!"
I must admit it was hard not to get excited about the Bahamas in the middle of winter.

We left for Detroit in a snowstorm and had to wait while the plane's wings were de-iced. I felt nervous, as usual, but everything went well, and we arrived safely at the Detroit airport. We spent the next two hours admiring the extraordinarily high hotdog prices before flying on to Fort Lauderdale.

We arrived around midnight and promptly missed the hotel shuttle, so we hailed a cab whose driver's English was difficult to understand. He mumbled something unintelligible and took us on a midnight tour of Ford Lauderdale before dropping us at our hotel at one o'clock in the morning. We fell into bed, secure in the knowledge that we'd have to be up again in four hours.

By 5:00 a.m., we were in the hotel lobby only to discover that the shuttle didn't run that early. Another cab was called, and while we waited, we counted our cash. Our two-hundred-dollar balance was dwindling rapidly: a hotdog here, a taxi there, and we were down thirty dollars.

At the harbour, we joined other yawning tourists filling out Bahamian customs declaration forms and lining up to be herded through various queues.
Jacqui had the brilliant idea that we should keep our luggage with us so we could get off the ferry faster when we arrived. This caused a number of traffic jams at the breakfast buffet where we looked like bag ladies burdened with suitcases, purses, and food trays.

No amount of coffee could resurrect us, and we decided it was time for a mid-morning nap in the sunshine. That

morning was exceptionally cold, so we sat on the deck of a Bahamian cruise ship wearing Canadian winter gear.
We were soon joined by other passengers who appeared incredulous when they learned we were from Canada.
"And you complain about the cold?"

We dozed off and were awoken frequently by hopeful waiters with gigantic neon-colored plastic cups brandishing palm trees and containing something called a Bahama Mama. Finally, Jacqui took pity on one of the waiters and after saying, "No, thank you," nine times, she ordered a rum laced concoction, while I ordered juice.

No sooner were we ready to resume our nap when the cruise manager announced a very important travel talk in the Starlight Lounge.
"You go," I said to Jacqui, "I'm too bushed."
For once, my older sister actually did what she was told, and while she was off getting educated about the Bahamas, I snuggled into my winter coat and went back to sleep.

I awoke two hours later to find that Jacqui was still missing.
Did she go overboard? Should I get up and find her?
While I was still drowsily debating the best course of action, she turned up with an ominous spring in her step and clutching a bunch of papers.
"What's all this?" I asked.
"Our agenda!" she said.

"Agenda? What is it you've got me doing this time?"

On our last trip, I went horseback riding, which left me in pain for two weeks.

"Tomorrow morning we're going on the Great Bahamian Getaway!" she said. "In the afternoon, we're snorkelling, and in the evening, we're at the Yellow Bird Native Show. Happy Birthday!"

I was too stunned to speak. "And when do we laze around on the beach?"

This trip was supposed to be relaxing.

"Sunday morning," she replied.

"And what am I doing Sunday afternoon?"

"We're doing the Dolphin Experience," she announced happily.

I did feel excited about the prospect of swimming with dolphins. This was something I had always wanted to do.

"So on Monday we're going to the beach, right?" I asked hopefully.

"Nope. We're going on the Lucayan National Park Tour."

Good-bye, beach.

A short time later, we made our way to the luncheon buffet feeling like a couple of refugees with our plastic bags, suitcases, and winter coats.

"Iron rations," Jacqui said, letting a couple of buns with cheese and meat fall into our luggage beneath the table.

We arrived in Freeport with a bang, literally. Still up on deck, we had a good view of the ferry's side. The captain had managed to do considerable damage during his parking efforts. Now that we were no longer moving, we could feel the sun's heat and were compelled to shed a few layers. It took a while to disembark, during which time our noses began to turn pink.

Finally, we were shuttled into a group taxi and carted off to the Island Palm Hotel in downtown Freeport. It was a different world driving on the left side of the road at neck-breaking speeds with no one buckled up, but I figured we were wedged in so tightly it didn't really matter.

As soon as we arrived, we changed into our bathing suits and lined up with other pale and tired tourists waiting for the shuttle to the beach.
"Since we only have three days, we might as well make the most of it," Jacqui said.
We were taken to the Island Palm's sister hotel and immediately felt like the visiting poor relations. We could be spotted a mile away. We were the ones without lounge chairs that cost four dollars each. I began to see why Jacqui had managed to get such a "good deal." This vacation package was the opposite of "all inclusive."

We stayed at the beach for only an hour. It was a sobering experience. The sand was full of broken shells and glass, the sun hid behind the clouds, and the wind was chilly. We returned to the hotel and decided to wash down our iron rations with two beers from the pool bar.

Overtired and giddy with beer, we fell into bed as soon as the sun had set.

The next morning, Jacqui remembered while showering that it was my birthday and shouted "Happy Birthday!" through the closed bathroom door.

A short while later, we went in search of breakfast and found it at the pool bar. It consisted of two runny eggs, greasy potatoes, bacon, and instant coffee served in Styrofoam cups. For this gourmet fare we forked out fifteen dollars and swore never to eat there again.

There wasn't much time to lament this breakfast, however, because the bus taking us on the Great Bahamian Getaway was waiting at the front gate. Our driver's name was David. He was not only our tour guide but also doubled as comedian, police officer, and volunteer firefighter. While driving us to various locations, he told us about the recent history of the Bahamas, preferred foods and their preparation, the island's religion, health and legal systems, its schools, prisons, and government.

We learned that in 2003, the majority of Grand Bahama was Baptist, and church was attended religiously (pardon the pun). Corporal punishment was still acceptable in the school system, and the death penalty by hanging was still practiced in the Bahamas at the time.

Our first stop was Grove's Botanical Garden, in honour of the Grove family who was instrumental in the development of Grand Bahama Island, especially Freeport. Thanks to Mr. Grove, people lived without property tax and much less poverty than in the Dominican Republic, for example.

The Botanical Garden was beautiful and we spent an hour feasting our eyes on sparkling waterfalls and lush green foliage with riotously colorful blossoms.

Next, David took us to the Banana Bay Restaurant on Fortune Beach. This beach made up for the other one. We ordered conch fritters and banana bread. Conch is a giant muscle and the favorite dish of the Bahamian people. Jacqui liked it, but I wasn't much for eating seafood-flavoured rubber. I relied heavily on the banana bread to satisfy my hunger.

"Jacqui, how come this banana bread tastes and looks so different from my homemade banana bread?" I asked. "Mine always has little black banana bits in it, and this one's just really yellow."

We looked at each other and started to laugh.

"Artificial banana flavour!"

Jacqui was determined to question our waitress when she brought the bill.

She laughed uncomfortably.

"Yeah, it has banana in it!"

"But it also has artificial flavour," Jacqui said. She was like a dog with a bone.

The waitress laughed again, but it sounded even more uneasy than before. She admitted to the artificial banana flavour in Banana Bay's famous bread. We packed the rest for iron rations. Fake or not, it was pretty good.

David took us next to the liquor wholesale and transformed into bartender and salesman. He let us sample the local flavoured rums: vanilla, banana (again), and pineapple while he rhymed off the recipes for Bahama Mamas and Yellow Birds. Jacqui and I felt woozy, either from the rum, the artificial flavours, or both.
The rum tasting was followed by a whirlwind tour of the fruit market and the international bazaar before David dropped us off at the snorkelling adventure destination.

We boarded a strange looking boat with two decks, a big yellow waterslide, and a climbing wall. While we headed out to the reef, we were furnished with fins, goggles, life vests, and fish food. I was concerned about the water temperature, but our guide and his sidekick assured us it would be around 78º F. This was definitely not what it had felt like earlier in the day when we had waded around Fortune Beach.

We stopped in the shallow waters of the reef.
"Don't touch the orange- or mustard-colored corals! If you do, the trip is over, and we'll take you to the hospital," our guide said.
Everyone scrambled to look over the side of the boat and see if they could spot the deadly corals.
"Better yet, don't touch anything!"

Thus reassured that this was a safe expedition, we put on our gear and jumped overboard.

Swimming was somewhat difficult with an underwater camera and a bag of fish food, which turned out to be dog kibble. Next time we go south, I must remember that I can save money by bringing my own dog food.

I lost sight of Jacqui almost instantly and decided to strike out on my own. There were flat, zebra-like fish, long, sleek blue fish with yellow fins and tail, dark blue ones that preferred to stay away from me, and black ones with neon blue stripes. I soon found myself surrounded by different schools of fish. I felt as if I were on the inside of a huge aquarium. In my excitement, I forgot my head was underwater.

"Jacqui—look!"

I got a snorkel full of salt water and a sudden pain in my leg, both reminders that I didn't belong here. I surfaced and gasped for breath before floating on my back to survey the damage to my leg. We had been warned that there were sharks in the water, but supposedly they were "puppy sharks," and since they had no teeth, the worst they could do was gum you to death. Upon closer inspection, I discovered I was not mortally wounded and carried on, a bit more cautious than before and no longer feeling as one with the fish.

In the meantime, Jacqui had made a sport of scattering her

kibble among the other members of our snorkelling expedition. Having a twisted sense of humour, she derived great pleasure in watching people yelp in surprise as fish jumped around their heads.

The waterslide opened up, and I found myself dodging flying bodies that came shooting out of the bottom of the sliding tubes. It was surely time to get back on board. While I inspected my leg, Jacqui tried the climbing wall. She actually had enough energy left.
My injury turned out to be a round, red sore about the size of a one-cent piece, with tiny, bleeding tooth marks. I didn't know fish had teeth. Jacqui thought it hilarious that I was the only one who got bitten while snorkelling. She made sure to tell every person on board, and I had to show my thigh to every one of the thirty strangers present.
Thank you, Jacqui!
"Just think," she said reassuringly, "if a little fishy can do this much damage, imagine what a dolphin could do to you!"

As soon as we were back at the hotel, it was time to get dressed for dinner at the Ruby Swiss. David had said: "All you have to do is stand at a bus stop and look lost. A bus will come along and pick you up. Tell the driver where you want to go, and he'll take you there, or to a stop close to it."
Hoping David hadn't been joking, we stood uncertainly at the nearest bus stop. Just as the bus arrived, so did a black

man dressed in a suit.

"Would you ladies have some change for me?"

Unfortunately, all we had was bills.

"Just hop on," Jacqui said. "We'll pay your fare with ours."

He thanked us, and handed her a note with his name and phone number.

"You've done me a kindness, and I would like to repay you. I'm a taxi driver, so when you need a ride to the harbour, you call me."

"You see," Jacqui said on the way to the restaurant, "Commit random acts of unexpected kindness and you'll never know what can happen."

At the Ruby Swiss, we treated ourselves to beef fondue with mushrooms and half a bottle of red wine before heading off to the Yellow Bird Club for the native show. There we met up with some familiar faces from the cruise ship and decided to join them. We each ordered a Yellow Bird and settled in to enjoy the performance.

Three native girls appeared and danced in colorful, risqué costumes to the music of a local band. One girl turned out to be a fire-eater. She licked the flame of her torch and lit the cigarette of an onlooker with her burning tongue. The next act was a limbo dancer who invited men from the audience to join him. A limbo competition followed, ending with the dancer carrying a ten-year-old boy with him as he squeezed under the limbo stick, his back a

hand's width off the floor.
"Thomas the Islander" ended the show by playing his steel drums, and the band bid us "Farewell and God Bless."

We shared a taxi with our new-found friends, thus keeping the cost down. Unfortunately, our share was six dollars, but we only had five.
"It's okay," the driver said, and we found ourselves at the receiving end of a random act of kindness.

In the hotel room, I ended my birthday with a nasty migraine brought on no doubt by too much flavoured Bahamian rum mixed with red wine. But I had a great birthday.
Thanks, Jacqui!

The next morning, we headed out to find breakfast, determined not to eat at our hotel ever again. Walking down the sunny sidewalk enjoying the quiet Sunday morning, we discovered a local restaurant, Geneva's, and decided to try our luck there. It was a charming place where the inhabitants of the island dropped in after church. We sat at a table in a sunny corner watching the locals as they talked and joked with each other across the room. We heard about their children's troubles at school or the gossip about mutual friends and discovered it's the same all over the world. Everyone wants to raise their children in peace and have enough money to look after them well.

We paid by credit card to preserve the little cash we had left and walked back to our hotel to spend a lazy morning, sunning, dozing, and reading by the very frigid swimming pool before heading off to our dolphin experience with UNEXSO in Port Lucaya.

Once again, we boarded a boat, but this one took us through one of the many man-made canals out to the open ocean where we picked up speed and flew across the aquamarine water towards the dolphin sanctuary. Twenty five years ago, UNEXSO had started with three dolphins, and the number had grown to fifteen with more calves on the way. The dolphins lived in an enclosed lagoon and were taken for outings into the open ocean, much like a dog would be taken out for walks. Sometimes, one or more would decide to join the wild dolphins and stay out for a while, but they always returned home to the sanctuary.

We were instructed to sit on a floating dock to observe two dolphins, Scarab and his "main squeeze," Lucaya, who was expecting his baby. The dolphins performed jumps for us and sprayed us with water while the trainer answered our questions.

Then it was time for us to climb into the enclosure and meet the dolphins in person. We stood on a platform in waist-deep water. Jacqui and I were in the second group of people, having decided to watch first. The water was freezing, but I was too excited to worry about it. Lucaya swam up between us, while Scarab surfaced on my left side. We were told to stroke the dolphins' backs and must have done a good job, because Lucaya turned over and offered us her swollen belly to rub. The cuddle session ended with Lucaya giving each of us a kiss.

Once we were out of the cold water, we discovered we were both hungry and thirsty. Jacqui spotted a coconut vendor at the corner, but when we arrived at his stand, we found it deserted. We looked around and were approached by a taxi driver in shirt and tie.
"You Ladies want a coconut?" he asked, and took off to find the owner of the stand.
He returned empty handed a short while later.
"He's gone home for the day," he said, taking a coconut and chopping it up with a machete he found under the stand. I had a vision of him cutting off his tie.
"Be careful!" I warned, remembering how my husband had needed stitches after his last encounter with a coconut. Luckily, no trip to the hospital was required, and our kind Samaritan offered us a drink from our coconut before going at it again with the machete and a paring knife.
"It's okay," Jacqui said. "We can do the rest. Thank you very much."
We paid the taxi driver who assured us he would pass the money on to the owner.

We took turns cutting the meat from the coconut and

were so absorbed in our activity we didn't see the police officer approaching. There he was in front of us, and it occurred to me that we had no proof the coconut we were butchering belonged to us. Then I remembered this country still had the death penalty.

"You, ladies, enjoying your coconut?" He smiled as if it were the most natural thing in the world to see us helping ourselves.

Two more security guards passed after that, and each time we were simply told to enjoy.

At the hotel, we changed into more respectable clothes and went in search of dinner. We returned to Geneva's and found it deserted with the exception of the waitress who sang along to a church program on the radio.

"Where is everybody?" Jacqui asked.

"In church," she answered and continued to sing.

By the time we were ready to leave, the church program was over and the restaurant had begun to fill with tourists and locals. At the time of our visit, Freeport had 45,000 inhabitants and about 500,000 tourists a year.

The next morning, we were off on the Lucayan National Park tour. As we climbed into the bus, we were greeted enthusiastically.

"Rejoice, for this is the day the Lord has made and we are spending it together!"

We drove through the more remote parts of Grand Bahama Island, passing a number of unfinished houses.

Our bus driver explained.

"In the Bahamas, you can build a house in stages over five years whenever you have some money. When you're done, you own your house and have no mortgage to pay."

Not bad, no mortgage, no taxes. What a wonderful concept!

We arrived at the Lucayan National Park and followed our guide to freshwater caves. He told us that the oldest son of the Lucayan Indians, who used to live on the island, was taught the knowledge of herbal medicine using local vegetation.

"I am the oldest son," he said, and proceeded to point from tree to shrub, telling us the local as well as the Latin name, and how the leaves, bark, and juice are prepared to heal anything from prostate cancer to diabetes. The man was a walking medical and herbal encyclopaedia.

We climbed down into the caves, and I knew we must be on sacred ground. Everyone was very quiet, and I suspected that I was not the only one feeling awed by our surroundings. Our guide broke the silence.

"One of the caves was used as a birthing place, while the other is a burial chamber."

The bottom of the cave was a body of freshwater that shimmered aquamarine in the semi-darkness.

We walked on and came to a swamp that we traversed using a boardwalk, which ended in a pine forest. The whole island used to be covered in pine groves until the government allowed the United States to log the island in the 1940s. Not much was left standing after the loggers were done. We walked through the forest and stopped in surprise. On the other side of the trees was the most beautiful beach I had ever seen. We had arrived at Gold Rock Beach, which was currently under low tide. It appeared to go on for many miles.

Jacqui jumped in for a swim, but I was content to wade through the shallow surf and feast my eyes on white sand and blue water. According to our guide, foreign investors were offering millions to the Bahamian government for this land, but so far the authorities had refused. This beach was completely untouched, and I hoped it would always remain this way.

On our way back, we visited a restaurant at Churchill Beach. Jacqui opted for more conch, this time in chowder form, while I made the mistake of ordering a Caesar salad with shrimp. I had to pay nine dollars for five tiger shrimp. I washed my salad down with a supersized pina colada while Jacqui tried a local concoction made with rum, of course.

As soon as we had returned to our hotel, it was time to call a taxi to drive us to the ship. Everyone else had already left. As usual, Jacqui had managed to make us late. If Brian, the cab driver for whom we had paid the bus fare, didn't come through, there was a good chance we would miss the ferry. We called him and he remembered us immediately.

"I'm not in my cab right now, but I'll be right over with my personal car."

True to his word, he arrived ten minutes later and drove us to the harbour. We wanted to pay him gas money, but he refused.

"You keep my number. If you ever come back, you call me."

On the cruise ship, we were determined to be less lethargic than we were on our first trip. This time we walked around, and I decided to take half of our remaining ten dollars to the casino. Maybe I could earn us enough money for breakfast the next morning. Alas, it wasn't meant to be. Ten minutes later, I was without my five dollars.

We agreed to keep the last of our money for the cab fare from the harbour to our hotel in Fort Lauderdale, but we made the mistake of sitting in the Starlight Lounge where there was a bingo tournament going on. Jacqui and I had never played before, and unfortunately, she chose this moment to decide that bingo was not meant to be a spectator sport. When they announced the final game of the evening, she held up our last five-dollar bill. The organizer came around to collect the money.

"What is Superjack Bingo?" Jacqui asked.

He took her money. "You need all the numbers."

We looked at each other blankly.

"There goes our ride to the hotel," I said.

We sat poised at the edge of our chairs with our bingo card between us, ready to poke holes into the little squares.

"B—36!"

"O—52!"

"B? O? Where are they getting these letters from?" Jacqui asked, looking bewildered.

This was especially amusing, considering that both Jacqui and I worked in information technology and considered ourselves to be fairly bright individuals.

"How many systems analysts does it take to poke holes into one bingo card?" I asked pointing to the word BINGO at the top of the card. Even with the two of us poking holes into the card at record speed, we were not the first ones to shout, "Bingo!"

We were now officially broke.

"No matter," Jacqui said, forever the optimist. "There's an ATM machine in the casino."

The machine turned out to be broken, but we were assured there was another in the main foyer. This contraption must have been the property of a loan shark because the charge to withdraw funds was eight dollars.

"No way!" Jacqui was livid. "Most taxis take credit cards. We'll just have to find one that does."

We enjoyed our buffet dinner included in the fare and

followed it up with a walk on deck until it began to rain. Drenched and windswept, we made our way into the Tropical Lounge to listen to karaoke. As we made our way to a small table by the dance floor, the organizer handed us a big black book with song titles.

Once we were seated, I noticed that the lounge was suspiciously quiet. It felt like the kind of quiet that falls across a room when someone asks for volunteers and everyone keeps their heads down to avoid eye contact. I turned to the table next to us.

"Where's the karaoke?" I asked.

"Here, but nobody's had the nerve to sing yet," said the young girl closest to me. "I think Mike and Mark are almost ready though."

She pointed to a collection of neon-colored cups on top of the table. I looked at the guys wearing a collection of miniature paper umbrellas on top of their baseball caps. At that moment, the organizer called their names, and they walked lopsidedly onto the dance floor. While they sang "Sweet Home Alabama," Jacqui continued to look through the black book.

"Hey, Annette! Look—they've got "I don't know how to love him" from Jesus Christ Superstar. You used to sing that!"

She got all excited, which was never good sign.

"Forget it!" I said. "That was over twenty years ago, and I don't know if I remember it."

As a teenager, I had driven everyone in the house crazy by

practicing this song for an audition. Part of me would have liked to sing it again, but surely not in front of a room full of people.

There was polite applause for "Sweet Home Alabama," sung simultaneously in two keys.

Next, two girls took heart and attempted a song by Cher. We were ten minutes from port and karaoke was coming to an end. Too bad, I would have liked to try, but I just didn't have enough nerve to go up and volunteer for this sort of thing. My performance anxiety was monumental and debilitating, complete with heart racing and knee knocking.

"We have time for one more performance," the organizer announced. "Annette will sing "I don't know how to love him," from Jesus Christ Superstar!"

Too bad Jacqui didn't have a camera. My face would have made a priceless shot. Somehow, she had managed to fill out the form behind my back and pass it to the lady next to us, who had taken it to the front.

"What?" I made the mistake of jumping up when I heard my name, giving Jacqui the opportunity to propel me across the dance floor with one swift, well-placed kick. The organizer handed me a microphone. There was no time to think.

"When do I sing?" I asked in confusion. She pointed to a TV screen.

"Now!"

I started to sing, but I couldn't hear myself. I heard only a voice coming strong and clear from all the speakers around the room, a voice I didn't recognize.

"Well, she's doing a good job," I thought, "I'll just sing along with her and everything will be fine."

I was so focused, I didn't hear people starting to whistle and applaud. I felt like I was in a deep haze. As soon as I realized the voice belonged to me, I started to feel nervous, but by this time, I was more than half way through the song. When I finished, everyone cheered and clapped. I looked over to Jacqui who was beaming at me.

"I think you may have cured my performance anxiety once and for all. If I can do this, I can do anything."

By the time the ship pulled into port, it was 10:30 p.m., and we were waiting to check out.

"If we can be in front of the building before eleven o'clock, we can catch the shuttle to the hotel," Jacqui said.

By the time we got outside, it was five minutes past eleven, and although the parking lot was teaming with shuttles, ours wasn't among them. It was raining buckets, and it didn't take long before we were drenched. Jacqui approached a cab and asked about payment by credit card.

"No, nobody takes credit cards," the driver replied and turned away from us to find a customer with cash.

Another cabbie offered to take us for twenty Canadian dollars, a sum that exceeded the US fare more than threefold.

I was wet and tired enough to give in.

"But there's got to be another way!" Jaqui said.

She made her way over to a pay phone and called the hotel.

"All set!" she announced a few minutes later.

She had sweet-talked the male receptionist into paying our cab fare and adding it to our hotel bill. Apparently, he couldn't stand the thought of two poor girls standing alone in the rain and darkness at the harbour front.

"Do you think he would have felt sorry for us knowing that we lost it all to bingo?" I wondered aloud.

The next morning found us sitting in a plane on route to Detroit beside a lady from Russia, who now lived in the city. She had a huge cardboard package at her feet, and I wondered how she got it passed the luggage check. As soon as the flight attendant spotted the package, she insisted that it be stored in an overhead bin. Since those above our seats were full, she squished it into the compartment across the aisle from us. Shortly after takeoff, the passengers seated under the bin looked up uneasily and began to gesticulate wildly at the flight attendant. When she opened the bin, a deluge of water poured down on the passengers below.

"Whose is this?" the attendant asked, looking around. She wasn't happy.

"Me," the Russian lady said.

"What is this?" the attendant asked. Her voice had an edge to it.

"Is a fish," the lady said in broken English, "Is ice."

The wet passengers started sniffing each other's wet clothes, while the flight attendant prepared to descend on our neighbor with murder in her eye.

"Well, you did tell her to put it up there," Jacqui said, coming to the fish owner's defence, forestalling any argument.

The attendant hesitated for a moment, clearly trying to decide whether to argue with Jacqui or find some blankets and a garbage bag. She opted for the latter, and the Russian lady breathed an audible sigh of relief.

By the time we reached Toronto, our mood had deteriorated. Our vacation had come to an end, and it was time to part ways. I was booked on a shuttle bus to Horseshoe Valley, and Jacqui would fly on to Ottawa. Little did we know that she would be stuck in Toronto for several more hours due to technical problems with her plane's front wheel.

We embraced and held each other tightly. It had been such a short trip, and yet we had experienced so much in the last few days. We felt very alive and much closer. We promised to see each other soon. Then she stepped onto the escalator, and I walked through the door back into a winter wonderland. There was a meter of snow on the ground and the temperature was a balmy minus fifteen degrees. There was no doubt.

I was home again.

Ostara

When my oldest daughter, Maya, returned from a trip to the library with a book on Wicca, my alarm lights went on. What was she into now? I wanted to approach this new direction with an open mind and borrowed the book. It didn't take me long to become intrigued with the Wiccan philosophy of "harm ye none." I read about rituals to honour nature, and since we were approaching Ostara, the spring equinox, I decided to perform a Wiccan planting ritual. It didn't sound too difficult and involved planting seeds with the ashes of a burnt piece of paper containing a wish.

As is the case with many best-laid plans, my ritual did not go off as described in the book. My first challenge was the fact that Ontario's spring equinox is in the middle of winter and the snow was still knee deep.

It must have taken me nearly ten trips and half an hour to cart all my stuff outside through the snow and to my tree stump, which was to be my altar. Some improvisation was needed, as I was, at best, only a gray witch without the tools of the trade.

The next problem was to read my notes by moonlight, and

luckily, with every candle lit, it got easier. Once my circle was cast, my smudge lit, and everything including me purified, I lit a candle for every Tower: East, West, South, and North, the Unity candle, and the God and Goddess candles. I stood in the front yard, hopefully hidden from the street, surrounded by candles stuck in the snow and three more on a tree stump.

I knelt down and discovered I had no paper to write on, so I had to rip a sheet out of my Grimoire, the most sacred book of shadows, to write my wish. The act of defiling my Grimoire, a fancy name for a Wiccan diary, somewhat broke the sacred moment, but not to be deterred, I got back to it, wrote my wishes (why stick to one with all this work?), and took wax from each Tower candle to seal them. So far, so good. Unfortunately, I had the bright idea of lighting my paper from all divine candles rather than just one. I figured there was strength in numbers.

Starting with the Goddess candle, I attempted to hold my paper in each flame. By the time I got to the Unity candle, the paper was completely engulfed. Rather than burning in my cauldron, the whole thing dropped into the Unity candle where it continued to burn, covered in wax. I thought longingly of the tongs I used to seize pickles from the pickle jar. Instead, I took my bundle of smudge and retrieved the burning wish from the Unity candle by flipping it into my brass mortar, which played the part of the cauldron. My Unity candle flickered and died.

The smudge I used was a cylindrical bundle of herbs tied with twine. It was supposed to last for months if used properly. Obviously, flipping burning wishes out of candles was not a proper use. Covered in wax, it went from smoldering to burning brightly like a torch. I wondered if my wish could still come true, if, during burning, it killed the Unity candle. I rekindled the candle with the burning smudge, putting more wax onto it in the process.

With respect to the element of fire, one was not supposed to blow out a flame, but my smudge burned dangerously close to my hand. How lucky for me that my altar was still surrounded by snow. As I wondered how disrespectful it would be, I stuck my burning smudge headfirst into a snow bank.

Now that the fire situation was under control, I could get back to the ritual. My next step was to plant the seeds and sprinkle them with the ashes from the wish. The planting went off without a hitch, but the sprinkling left something to be desired. My ashes wouldn't sprinkle, instead big gobs of wax plopped onto my newly planted seeds.

I finished as I should, extinguishing my candles, thanking the Towers, the God and the Goddess, and hoped they had a sense of humour. I completed the ritual by lifting the circle and indulging in a sip of red wine.

This was followed by two more glasses once I had carted everything back into the house. I surveyed the damage I had inflicted on my seeds by planting them in hot wax. Maybe I should have wished I hadn't killed my seeds with the ritual. I decided that even though Wicca is an intriguing philosophy, I should probably stick to reading about it.

If this wish ever comes true, it will be a miracle. But that's what it's supposed to be all about, isn't it?

Blessed be!

Family Reunion

In the nineties, I was employed as a systems consultant at a large brokerage company in Toronto. As there were many contractors working together, we shared an office. One day, the computer network was down and we found ourselves without work for some time. Although we had worked together and knew each other's names, we had never taken the time to get to know one another. It turned out we were an international group from all over the world: India, Pakistan, Iraq, Germany, Bosnia, Serbia, United States, and Canada.

When the introductions were over, a hush fell over the room. It occurred to us that unlike some of our countries of origin, we were not only able to get along peacefully but could work together and be productive as a group.

The conversation soon turned to the question of how each of us had come to Canada. Some had arrived as refugees and others were sponsored by family. One young man had an extraordinary story to tell.
"Even though I grew up in Iraq, I was actually born in Germany."
"Wait a minute, Randy" I said, "I thought you were from the United States."

He smiled. "I moved to the States when I was a teenager, but I was born in Germany. My mother is German, but I haven't seen her since I was a young boy."

He pulled out his wallet and handed me a small black and white photograph that showed a young woman with a shy smile and large glasses. I turned the picture over to see if I could find a date stamp but found instead handwritten German words. I read them quietly and felt a lump forming in my throat. I looked up at Randy who was watching me expectantly.

"Do you know what this means?" I asked him. He shook his head. "What?"

I hesitated then translated. "My heart will always be with you."

He took the photograph from my outstretched hand and turned away, but I had seen the tears in his eyes. The room became very still as we watched him carefully return the picture to his wallet.

"I was born the year the Berlin wall was built," he said. "When I was six months old, my father took me across the border, just before it closed, leaving my mother behind in East Berlin. My aunt came from Iraq and helped my father look after me, but my Iraqi relatives kept pleading with him to go back to East Germany and get my mother. As Iraqi citizens, they were allowed to cross the border.

"Finally, three months later, my uncle and my father hollowed out the back seat of a car and smuggled my mother into West Germany. My aunt stayed with us for close to a year, before she went back to Iraq. She couldn't stand my parents' constant fighting and hoped that in her absence they would unite over the task of caring for me.

"After a few months, my father took my mother and me to live in Iraq, but she was desperately unhappy and tried to run away with me. Eventually, my father gave in, and we moved back to Germany, but I missed my aunt. To me, she was my mother.

"When it became obvious to my parents that the marriage was over, my father took me, without my mother's knowledge, and handed me over to a business associate who was flying to Iraq. He was to deliver me to my aunt. I was three years old, and I never saw my mother again."

A long silence followed.
"Have you ever tried to find her?" I asked.
"I have her address."
"And?"
"I wrote, but she has never answered. Perhaps because my father did the translating and God knows what he wrote."
I hesitated again before speaking. "If you ever want to try again, I'll be happy to translate for you."
"I'll think about it," he said, and that was the end of the conversation.

Months went by during which I couldn't get Randy's story out of my head. How would I feel if one of my children were taken from me? How his mother must have suffered, lying awake at night, thinking about her little boy growing up so far from her.

Mother's Day came, and Randy asked me to write a letter. We included a photograph of his son who was the same age he had been the last time his mother had seen him.
Spring turned to summer, summer to fall, and still no word from Germany. Why wouldn't she answer? Perhaps it had taken so much time and effort to bury the past that she didn't want to open old wounds. Randy was ready to give up, but I told him not to.
"Let's keep writing. I'm sure she'll answer you, when she feels ready."
We sent a Christmas card and there was no answer.

In the spring of the following year, Randy's father passed away.
"Perhaps your mother was afraid of your father. Let's write to her again."
We waited until the fall before we wrote another letter. I didn't think he expected a response any longer when it finally came. It was eight o'clock on a December evening, when my phone rang. His breathless voice shouted into my ear.
"I got a letter from Germany, but I can't read it!"
We lived an hour's drive apart, so I couldn't simply jump into the car and drive over.
"Can you read it to me?" I asked.
Randy tried, but his pronunciation was so bad I couldn't

make sense of anything. He decided to drive the letter over to a friend who owned a scanner and e-mail it to me. I waited for almost an hour before my phone rang again.

"Okay, I sent it to you," he said. "Call me back when you've got it."

I opened my email and there it was. I looked at the closed message and felt excited and afraid. What if Randy's mother had written that she didn't wish any contact with him? Perhaps she really did want to forget the past, and I would have to hurt Randy's feelings. My hand trembled as I pushed the mouse across the pad and clicked to open the email.

My dear Son,
I am sorry it took me so long to answer your letters and I'm glad you kept writing. It wasn't easy for me. I had to tell your brother and sister about you, but now that I have done it, I'm glad I did. They are very excited to meet you. I have enclosed a photograph, so that you can see your family in Germany.
I hope to hear from you soon.
Love, your mother.

Relief washed over me, but I had to wait to call Randy. I was sobbing and couldn't speak. When I regained my composure, I picked up the receiver and dialed Randy's number.

"What did she write?"

I translated the letter.

"Photograph? What photograph? Oh no! I must have lost it outside when I opened the letter!"

He dropped the receiver and ran outside into the snow. I heard a door slam in the distance and footsteps hurrying towards the phone.

"I got it!" he said. "Who are the people in the picture? Did she say?"

"They are your brother and his wife, your sister with her kids, and your mother with her brother."

There was silence as he looked at his new family. I wished I could have seen the picture. Over the next few months, I continued to translate emails and letters for him. His brother came for a visit the next spring, and in the summer, his mother came to Canada to meet her son and his family.

Two years later, he took his wife and children to Germany where he met his uncles and aunts who had last seen him as a baby. The entire family met him at the airport with thirty years' worth of presents.

Upon his return, he sent me a big bouquet of flowers with a card.

"You are my Angel. Thank you!"

Blue Milk and Green Water

I'm not sure when or how this custom started at our place, but the first day of April is one I don't look forward to. It started harmlessly enough, with Dad tying up the kids' shoelaces and me adding food color to their morning milk. But every year the pranks escalated until we had an outright April Fools' War, complete with warring parties, namely, my husband, Pieter, and oldest daughter, Maya, and innocent bystanders as collateral damage.

It began just past midnight, when my youngest awoke shouting.
"Mommy! Mom...help!"
I awoke and rolled over onto my other side, still foggy.
"Mom!"
This call sounded more desperate, and I stumbled sleepily into Nadia's room to find her duct-taped, mummy style, to her bed. This had to be Maya's handiwork.
I loosened Nadia from her predicament and duct-taped my nightgown to her bedspread in the process. As soon as I had freed both of us, I stormed into Maya's room to find her peacefully asleep. I went back and kissed Nadia, reassuring her.
"Well, at least you've got it behind you. She got you while you were asleep, so I think you're safe now."

I went back to bed and noticed my husband had gone missing. His specialty was to get the entire family with one prank and keep Maya in check by barricading her room.

"Whatever," I grumbled to myself as I climbed back into bed. I was determined not to get involved this year and went back to sleep, but not for long.

A tremendous crash was followed by a scream. I recognized the voice of my second child, Lucia, and went in search of the new calamity. There she sat in her bed with the entire contents of her bookshelf. Pieter had used it to barricade Maya's adjoining bedroom door in an effort to confine her to her room and keep the collateral damage to a minimum. As with many well-laid plans, this one had backfired, literally.

I rescued my second child, the avalanche victim, from being held prisoner in her own bed. Two family members down and three to go.

I entered Maya's room to put a stop to this nonsense, but she was nowhere to be seen. Instead, I found my husband making Maya's bed. This was highly unusual. Pieter is not a man who frequently takes the initiative when it comes to housework, especially not at 3:00 a.m.

"What are you doing?"

He put a finger to his lips, took my hand, and tip-toed us back to our bedroom.

"What's going on?"

"Just a little surprise for Maya when she comes back from booby-trapping the rest of the house."

As if on cue, there was another bang followed by a shriek and a satisfied chuckle from Pieter.

"Let's go see," he said, cheerfully hopping out of bed.

I trailed behind with much less enthusiasm. At this point, my feet felt like ice cubes and my head like a smashed pumpkin. Still, I have to admit that the sight of Maya, terror of the family, folded in half like a Swiss army knife, was refreshing. She had the tendency to take a running jump into her bed, and her father had used her habit as a tactical advantage by removing the wooden slats of her bed frame. As Maya entered her bed at full speed, the mattress had collapsed beneath her. With both ends sticking up vertically, she found herself effectively pinned.

"I'll get you for this!" she said, trying to extract herself from the bed.

This was my cue to exit. I wanted no part in this. All I wanted was my bed and a few more hours of peaceful slumber before the alarm clock went off.

It did that at 6:00 a.m., and I could hardly open my eyes. I made my way to the bathroom and sat down on the device not often mentioned in literature, only to jump up again as if stung by a bee—not a bad comparison as the sensation was quite similar. On close inspection, I found that the toilet seat had been treated to a liberal application of Vick's VapoRub. As might be imagined, I was in fine spirits for the remainder of the morning.

But, we were not done yet. When I came into the kitchen, I got a handful of Vaseline from the light switch only to find that the lights stayed off, no matter how often I flicked the switch. Was Ontario Hydro participating in the April Fools' ceremonies at my house?
Good-bye hot coffee—and I really needed you this morning.

I decided on a breakfast of cereal and bent down, rummaging around my darkened fridge for the milk. It was cornered by a jug of water, and I had to retrieve both before I could straighten up. There I was, standing in my kitchen at six o'clock in the morning, holding a jug filled with green water and another with blue milk. You know what they say about the last straw? This still wasn't it.

We rushed through breakfast and sent the kids outside to catch the school bus. After some ten minutes, they came back inside.
"Mom, the bus didn't come. We must have missed it!"
That's when I noticed my husband's expression. He had a devilish gleam in his eye.
"What did you do now?"
The entire family turned to look at Pieter, who was well aware of the spotlight.
"Well, I think it's time the power came back on. Don't you feel like having a nice cup of coffee, Dear?"

I stared at him, incredulous and at a loss for words. He got up from the breakfast table and walked, whistling, to the basement door, descending into darkness. Within seconds, the lights came on, and we could hear him.

"Looks like someone's tripped the main breaker."

"Good one, Dad!" Maya laughed, "I have to remember that one for next year."

"You can't use that one again. It's against the rules."

Rules? There were rules of combat for April Fools' Day?

He rejoined us in the dining room and looked at his watch.

"Well, girls, I think it's time for you to go outside and catch your bus."

"But Dad, we missed it. Look at the time!"

Lucia pointed at Grandma's antique clock on the wall. He walked over to the clock and studied it closely.

"Funny," he said, "it's the first time ever that it's half an hour fast."

He turned to me with a big grin. "Dear, I think you'll have time for that cup of coffee after all."

"What? You mean it's not eight o'clock?"

"No, it's just past seven thirty. Maya, put on your coat; it's cold outside."

Our oldest was dumbstruck, but only for a moment as what her father had done sank in.

"Wow, Dad! I bow to greatness—you win! The power and

the clocks— that's great."

He feigned modesty. "I've long since done away with crude jokes like cream on light switches, tying shoelaces, or sewing up sleeves."

Just at that moment, Maya tried to slip her arm into her coat, but her hand struck resistance.

"Having trouble, Maya?" he asked innocently.

She took off her coat and examined the sleeve closely.

"Done away with the crude jokes, eh Dad?"

I shook my head. Thank heaven April Fools comes around only once a year.

I kissed the kids good-bye and went to the kitchen to make coffee. Pieter came in a short while later, placing his arm around me and taking a big sniff.

"Smells heavenly," he said.

"You sit down and I'll bring you a cup. You've had such a busy night."

Suspecting no evil from his loving wife, he strolled into the dining room. I followed him with two cups of steaming coffee. As I put his cup in front of him, he recoiled.

"What's that?"

"Why it's coffee, Dear, made with blue milk and green water."

Hero

Dancing had always been part of my life before motherhood changed my priorities, but when my children were old enough to start ballet lessons, I found myself wanting to dance again. Every time I dropped my girls off at their class, I heard loud music and stomping coming from the studio next door.

One day, I found the door slightly ajar and curiosity got the better of me. I peeked inside and saw women ranged in age from teenager to senior citizen, all wearing white shoes with double-metal clickers. I was hooked on clogging from the first moment I laid eyes on the dancers, all hooting, hollering, and stomping to the music. Being a shy individual, I didn't want to embark on this venture alone. I hesitated for about a year, trying to entice every one of my female acquaintances to join me for clogging lessons. Nobody was interested. Finally, I put trepidation aside and registered for beginners' class.

I was instantly welcomed and found the cloggers to be a close-knit and helpful group, especially two you teenagers, who turned out to be brother and sister. and Shawna were amazing dancers and it was a r watch them. As they became older, they charity events and variety shows. Everyone loved to watch them dance. Neither the start of high school nor part-time work kept them from attending their weekly clogging lessons. Dancing was their life.

At the start of last year's session, our teacher, Denise, announced that she had something special planned. She nodded at Shane and Shawna, who stepped out onto the dance floor, before she continued.
"While the rest of us were off on summer vacation, these two kept dancing and choreographed Shawna's favorite song, "Hero," which they will perform, and then teach you."
"We've dedicated it to Denise," Shawna said, blushing slightly.

They danced. The steps were intricate and well thought out, complementing the music perfectly. The two danced separately and then partnered up for the refrain, "I can be your hero," with Shane swinging his sister in and out, twirling her around his back and into position beside him. When they finished, we applauded wildly. Denise smiled at her protégés, who beamed with pride. Then it was our turn to learn the steps and swing each other around. There was more than one sore toe that night.

The following week, Shane was by himself and continued to teach "Hero," using Denise as a partner.
"Where is Shawna?" I asked.

He was strangely quiet. "She's sick."
I didn't want to pry, yet I was worried it might be more than a cold that had kept Shawna away that night.
When the next week came, and Shane was still by himself, he could no longer avoid the crowd of worried cloggers pressing to know more.
"Where's Shawna? What's wrong with her?"
"She's in hospital undergoing some tests. She fainted in the bathroom at school and hit her head on the sink. They think that she's got epilepsy or something."
The class continued with Shane and Denise.

The following week, Shawna returned—in a wheelchair. Tests had revealed she had contracted a brain virus that had caused her to lose all sense of balance. At fifteen, she was as helpless as a toddler when it came to standing on her own two feet. She looked pale, and her youthful, innocent face carried a trace of her recent pain and suffering. She sat, watching us dance. I had a hard time concentrating on my feet, wondering how she must feel seeing Denise dance her part.
"I can be your hero, baby/I can kiss away the pain."
I looked over at Shawna and saw tears in her eyes. My heart went out to her and her mother, who stood solemnly beside her.

The weeks went by with Shawna spending a good deal of time in physiotherapy learning to regain her balance. The wheelchair parked inside the door of the dance studio became a familiar sight. Denise had given up teaching us "Hero." Like the rest of us, she probably felt it was too painful for Shawna to watch.

After Christmas, Shawna surprised us.
"Look what I can do," she said to Denise, pulling herself up onto her brother.
She managed to stand and take a small, unsure step. We all crowded around her, shouting our congratulations.

With each week that passed, she proudly demonstrated her progress. Shane helped her in and out of the chair. Before we knew it, the time had come to part ways for another summer's dancing sabbatical. Shawna stood by the door with one arm around her mother's shoulder for support. Denise wished us all a happy and safe summer.
"See you in September," she said, hugging each of her students.
Shane waited in line. He whispered something into her ear.
"Are you sure?"
He nodded and went over to his sister. He took her by the arm and led her to the dance floor. She tried to pull away, but she couldn't leave the security of his firm grip.
"I can't, Shane," she said. There was a quaver in her voice.
"Yes, you can!" he said.

The music started. She carefully began moving her feet with, Shane dancing beside her and holding her arm, watchful not to disturb her fragile balance. I looked from them to their mother, who had worked so hard to help her daughter learn to walk for a second time. I could only imagine how she felt seeing her girl dance again after months in a wheelchair. How proud she felt of Shane and his infinite patience for his sister. I watched him as he cautiously guided Shawna around to the music of Enrique Iglesias:

I can be your hero, baby,
I can kiss away the pain,
I will stand by you forever,
You can take my breath away.

My Royal Experience

The special day had finally arrived. The Cottage Country Cloggers Show Team was the opening number at the Welcome to Ontario Festival in Honour of the Queen's Golden Jubilee. This meant that the royals would miss our performance, since we were to dance at three thirty, and they would not arrive until 6:00 p.m, but I was nervous nevertheless. After all, they were expecting around eight thousand visitors and dignitaries at this event.

As always, I got out of bed at 6:00 a.m. and spent the morning feeding animals, making breakfast, preparing lunches and driving kids to school. I got back home by nine thirty and began my transformation from stressed mother and housewife to glamorous performer. My hair went up in a bun with gold ribbons and sparkle. The dark circles under my eyes, from lack of sleep due to my snoring husband, were carefully hidden by numerous applications of makeup and powder.

By 11:00 a.m., the transformation was complete and the garment bag packed with all my essentials. With a parting look in the mirror confirming that I could no longer recognize myself, I left home in plenty of time to catch the limousine bus that our group had chartered for the drive to Toronto.

Driving down Highway 400 to Barrie, I recited the contents in my bag: black shoes–check; black skirt–check; black tights–check; black bodysuit–check; gold top, gold choker, gold earrings–check; invitation . . . invitation?

I left the highway at the closest ramp and entered it again moments later, reversing direction. When I got back home, my dogs didn't even bother to get up and greet me. Dumbledore lifted his head and gave me a tired look that said: "Oh, it's you again. What did you forget this time?"

I finally made it to Barrie, feeling like the stressed housewife again and had to look into the mirror once more to make sure I didn't look like I felt. Luckily, the bus trip to Toronto was uneventful and helped smooth my ruffled feathers, but it did nothing for the butterflies in my stomach.

When the bus deposited us at the National Trade Centre, there was a palpable excitement in the air. We lined up at the door where our numbered invitations were being checked, and we were given an exhibitor's pass, which we had to wear around our necks.
At two thirty, all doors were locked, and we were herded into Hall B while the RCMP did a security sweep of Hall A. Then it was off to the change rooms and the stage.

It's said that waiting is the hardest part, and I can attest to the truth of the statement. We lined up by the side of the stage subjected to curious looks from the audience during the completion of the sound check. People filtered in and filled the seats. Two security guards took up position on either side of the stage, and media filed in behind them.

"Ladies and Gentlemen! From the Centre Stage Studio – the dynamic, high stepping, energetic show team – The Cottage Country Cloggers!"

I felt a burst of adrenalin and the butterflies in my stomach took flight. We had only fifteen minutes to make an impression. The music and the pounding of our feet carried through the hall and drew an ever-increasing crowd of people. Those too far away from the stage looked up at the viewscreens to see what was going on.

Our performance went off without a hitch, and we received a good amount of applause. Mission accomplished! Now we were free to view the other displays and wait for the Queen. We changed out of our bodysuits and back into our embroidered white jackets with the red maple leaf. After watching the National Ballet and Stratford performances, we decided to line up along the red carpet that outlined the route the royal couple would take. Situated across from the police and service dogs, we figured we were in the perfect spot. The Queen was bound to stop here.

Teenage members of our group stood beside me and read from the protocol document we had received: "Take the royal hand only when offered. Do not subject it to vigorous pumping and return intact to its owner."

The teens continued to bob up and down, practicing their courtsies and checking their makeup, their efforts hindered by the flowers they held.

"Your attention please! The royal couple is only minutes away. Please extend a warm welcome when they enter the building."

This announcement was made several times during the next half hour. My feet were beginning to ache, and I was glad I had decided against my new high-heeled shoes and had opted for an old but comfortable suede pair with coffee stains. Who was going to look at my feet after I finished dancing?

Loud applause erupted at the other end of the hall, and the Queen and Prince Phillip could be seen on the viewscreen. The teens beside me jumped up and down with excitement, nervously twisting their flowers. The Queen came closer. The red carpet remained empty. Any minute now she should come around the corner. More police and security guards began to appear, including an RCMP officer at the head of a pyramid of security. Three rows of police were followed by photographers and media personnel trying to push each other out of the way, loudly juggling for position and the best shots.

I managed to briefly spot the top of the Queen's head when a solid line of police formed in front of us. I stood on tip toes and strained my neck. All I saw were police.

I looked up at the viewscreen that showed the Queen taking flowers from a little girl in a wheelchair. She approached the police dogs and was less than ten feet away from us, but all we still saw were police.

The teens beside me became restless. How were they going to give the Queen their mangled flowers? One of them accidentally put a foot forward onto the carpet and was immediately admonished by an officer. Her lower lip started to quiver. The Queen moved on. The police moved on. The girls were close to tears.

At that moment, an elderly gentleman in a suit approached us and stopped in front of the teens.

"Did you want to give her your flowers? Come on with me, Dear. Come on."

The three started forward, stammering about not being allowed on the red carpet, but the gentleman assured them it was all right to go with him. He brought them through the lines of police and told them to stand behind the Queen. Then he turned back towards me.

"Thank you so very much, sir," I said. "That means a lot to them."

He walked back to me, and I had a chance to take a good

look at him. My heart jumped. The man I had thanked was no other than Prince Phillip himself. He put an arm around my shoulder.

"What does it say on the back of your jacket?"

My jacket had been one of the later acquisitions and was not embroidered.

"Actually, nothing," I replied. "But it's supposed to say 'Cottage Country Cloggers.'"

I turned to my team member who stood next to me.

"Can you show your jacket?"

She had taken hers off and slung it over her arm. Recognizing the Prince, she dropped her purse, her protocol document, and her jacket on the floor.

"Cloggers?" asked Prince Phillip.

"Yes, it's a form of dancing."

He bent down to study the coffee stains on my shoes.

"Uh, those are not my dancing shoes. I took them off a while back, after we danced. You missed us."

"Oh, I see," he said, and walked back to the Queen, who had turned to the teens behind her.

All I could see now were their bobbing heads. They had begun to courtesy and forgotten to stop. Prince Phillip took one of the girls by the shoulders and turned her, so the Queen could read the back of her jacket.

"Look, Dear," he said, "They are clog dancers."

As the cameras attempted to zoom in on the Queen, all that was seen on television was the back of the teen's jacket. The screen was filled with the words "Cottage

Country Cloggers."

Later that evening, I had a chance to hear the reporters on national television.
"Now what do you suppose are Cottage Country Cloggers?"
There was a long silence.
"They're dancers . . . and they wear cool jackets."
This was followed by a longer silence, during which the screen continued to show the backs of our jackets, and someone scrambled to find information about our group.
"They're a dance group from Barrie, and they dance to Celtic, Gospel, Country and Rock'n'Roll music," the first reporter said. He had obviously found our web site.
They both heaved a sigh of relief when the Queen moved on.

When the teens returned to the side of the red carpet, reporters honed in on them, holding microphones in their faces.
"You just met the Queen. What was that like?"
The girls couldn't answer. One cried, another laughed, and the third still bobbed up and down.

I was interviewed about my conversation with Prince Phillip and my views on security at such an event. No sooner was the limelight off our faces then the Mayor of Barrie arrived on the scene to shake our hands. This is the same man who didn't have the time of day for us when we requested financial assistance with transport costs to the royal shindig. Now he offered us the once-in-a-life time-chance to ride on his float in the Barrie Santa Clause Parade.

We followed the Queen and congregated at the other end of the hall, where she was welcomed by Premier Eves and presented with a special video showing Ontario's development over the past fifty years. It was an emotional moment as it showed clips of the building of the CN tower, Terry Fox running, night-time campfires, and the Canadarm in Space. Premier Eves announced Ontario's new Queen Elizabeth Provincial Park and the Golden Jubilee Award for Bravery.

After the ceremony, we waited until the royal couple had safely departed the building before the rest of us were permitted to leave.

The next morning, it was back to making breakfast, preparing lunches, shuttling kids to school, and arriving at work barely in time. Only yesterday, I had been decked out in gold and glitter, socializing with royalty.

As I stood in the coffee lineup at work, someone tapped me on the shoulder. I turned and looked into the face of a smiling stranger.

"Yesterday you were on national TV, and today you're back in the coffee line with the rest of us mere mortals. Goes to show that even famous people are just people."

Famous?

She couldn't possibly be talking about me. Could she?

The Hornet

We were all gathered comfortably around the TV for family movie night when a huge hornet landed on Pieter's pant leg. Screaming kids scattered everywhere while I ran to fetch him a glass and a thin book. He carefully slipped the book underneath his pant leg and the glass over top.

He proceeded to show me how this angry insect tried to sink its stinger into the book. The kids came back to take a cautious look before we all escorted Pieter and his pissed-off hornet to the front door. As soon as he was outside, we slammed the door shut, sending him to do battle on his own, while we ran over to the window to support him from the safety of the living room.

Instead of leaving the book, glass, and incarcerated hornet on the patio table, Pieter took it for a walk and ended up in front of the open window. This is where he decided to give it freedom. Thank God for screen windows.

It was still busy stinging the glass and missed the opportunity to fly away. Again, it would have been prudent to put the glass down gently and retreat, but my brave and foolish husband shook the glass with the intention of dislodging the hornet and dumping it into a bucket of water conveniently located under the open window.

There was a lot of shouting, mainly profanity, as he performed amazing acrobatics.
"What's happening?" I asked.
"It's flying at me!"
"Then run!"
I didn't have to tell him twice.

He ran around the house to the front door. I had to scatter kids and dog to get to the door and open it. In his haste, he almost fell up the stairs, taking two at once and looking over his shoulder, panic stricken. The door closed and he kept going until he was in the safety of the living-room.
"Did you get stung?"
"It came flying at me."

Suddenly, he shot straight up into the air and hollered. Kids flew backwards, and he jumped from one foot to another while trying to rip off his sweater.
The hornet was firmly attached to it and busy stinging his back. As soon as he had freed himself from his sweater, he threw it to the ground and jumped on it with both feet, half naked and yelling with primeval ferocity while the hornet calmly watched from the living-room window.

"There it goes!" Nadia shrieked, as Dumbledore, our oversized family dog, entered the fray and attempted to catch the hornet, but Pieter had armed himself with a fly swatter. Stumbling over the dog, he caught up with the hornet and beat the tar out of it.

I'm happy to say that the window survived the onslaught. The hornet, however, was not so lucky, thus ending another relaxing family movie night.

The 13th Wedding Anniversary

As with many parents of young children, it wasn't often we got a chance to go away for a weekend. Therefore, it was a pleasant surprise when Pieter's parents agreed to take our three girls. When he and I were first married and without much money, we had spent our honeymoon in a tent in Algonquin Park. In an attempt to rekindle those memories, we decided to spend our thirteenth wedding anniversary canoeing in Killarney Park. We should have taken off our rose-colored glasses and done a better job of remembering that our honeymoon included a torrential rainfall and wet sleeping bags.

Forgetting that we were now thirteen years older and both working in sedentary occupations, Pieter planned our canoe trip. He had found a locally made cedar canoe at a garage sale and was itching to give it a test paddle. He also purchased a new set of backpacks that could hold up to eighty pounds each. I had visions of toppling over and lying on my back with my legs up in the air like a helpless bug.

The morning of our departure arrived. The kids were safely ensconced at the grandparents who had received a long list of instructions we knew would be ignored. We were off at last. Our plan was to drive to Killarney and spend the first night in the main park before heading into the interior the next day. The weather forecast promised sunny skies and we were in great spirits.

When we arrived at the park, the path to our assigned camp ground was barricaded by a sign: Do Not Enter – Campground Closed Due to Mother Bear and Cubs. We drove back to the park office to receive new marching orders and campsite information.

Once our tent was pitched and the cooking fire lit, I began our dinner preparations. For the first night, I had brought a couple of steaks, potatoes, and fresh vegetables. At least we would have one good meal. Once we were on our canoe trip, we would have to rely on our newly purchased fishing rods, beginners' luck, and some dry goods in case the fish decided not to bite.

The delicious scent of frying meat wafted through the campground, and it crossed my mind that cooking steak on an open fire may not be the wisest action if there were a bear around. No bear came to visit, however, and we enjoyed a wonderful meal. After the dishes were done and the sun had set, I sat at the picnic table with a cup of tea and a bag of oatmeal cookies.

Lost in thought and at peace with the world, I was about to bite into a cookie when someone gently touched my back. My first thought was that Pieter was trying to get my attention, but when I looked up, he was kneeling by the tent with his back to me. I felt paralyzed by fear, convinced that if I turned around, I'd be facing a bear. I tried to call Pieter's name, but no sound came out. I forced myself to look over my shoulder and found absolutely nothing. My gaze fell lower, and to my surprise, a racoon sat behind me, his paw outstretched about to touch my back again. But now he reached out and took the cookie out of my hand. Then he turned and disappeared, leaving me open-mouthed and empty-handed.

The next morning, Pieter woke me with a finger to his lips.
"Shhhh . . . be really quiet, and put your shoes on."
"What's going on?" I whispered.
He pointed to the half-open tent flap. There in front of us was mama bear visiting our next-door neighbors, who were crammed into their station wagon. Their faces were pressed against the windows, watching the bear kick their cooler across the campground. I heard a rustling in the tree next to our tent where the bear cubs were doing their morning chin-ups while the neighbor's dog circled.

Pieter and I silently put on our running shoes in case the situation demanded a sudden sprint. Thankfully, after ten minutes of fruitless effort, the bear gave up on the cooler, chased the dog away from the tree, retrieved her cubs, and went on her way. There was a collective sigh of relief.

When we felt certain the bear was gone, we began to pack up and get ready for our canoe trip. Breakfast would have to wait. We didn't want to tempt the bear into returning. Our gear stowed, we set off on our journey to David Lake where another campsite awaited us.

We had to traverse three lakes and two portages. It didn't take long to discover our new canoe was temperamental and not very forgiving when either of us shifted our weight without first alerting the other to counterbalance. Luckily, the combined weight of passengers and gear helped to keep us fairly stable.

Midway, we pulled up to a small island for lunch before tackling our first portage. To our delight, this was a short distance of railway track furnished with a platform designed to house a canoe. All we had to do was to heave our fully loaded canoe up onto it and then pull it along the track to the next lake.

We continued paddling, now with less enthusiasm and increasingly sore arms.
Happy to take a break, we approached the second portage. Our relief was short- lived. This portage didn't boast a railway track. Instead it had a steep path leading into the forest.
Pieter lifted my pack so that I could strap myself in. After fourteen kilometers of paddling, I wasn't nearly as strong

as I had been in our kitchen when we had tested the weight of the pack. I swayed ominously, and it became instantly apparent that he would have to carry the canoe by himself. We made it halfway, at which point we had to abandon gear in the middle of the forest to avoid collapse. This meant we walked the portage more than once.

By the time we made it to the shores of David Lake, the sky had become overcast and the wind had picked up. We reloaded the canoe and set off to find our campsite. There were a total of ten campsites on David Lake, clearly marked with red tipped stakes.
Unfortunately, whenever we spotted such a stake, we also saw a campfire burning, a sure sign that the site was occupied.

The sky grew darker and the waves higher. Exhausted from paddling, it became increasingly difficult to keep the canoe pointed into the waves. We began to rock dangerously from side to side. We needed to get off the lake fast and decided to find a shallow section of shore that would permit us to pull up the canoe and make camp. Then we could find our proper campsite the next morning in daylight.

It was almost dark by the time we found a suitable spot to pitch our tent. Covered in dirt and sweat, we took a swim before bed, which turned out to be an exceedingly bad idea. The windswept water was freezing and caused my sore muscles to spasm. I awoke in the middle of the night in excruciating pain.

The next morning was bright and sunny. I revived us with hot coffee and breakfast while we discussed whether to remain illegally camped or search for our assigned site. The debate ended when Pieter went to inspect some wild blueberry bushes nearby and unearthed a broken, red-tipped stake. This suited us perfectly. Still exhausted from the previous day's travel, we had no desire to move camp. We spent the next couple of days recovering and gathering strength for the return journey.

Meanwhile, on the home front, calamity had struck in the form of a hazelnut-laced chocolate candy. When Nadia was two years old, we discovered she was deathly allergic to nuts. Her reaction grew stronger with every exposure. By the time Nadia was five years old, she had been exposed on multiple occasions. Aware of the risk, Pieter's mother had carefully combed her kitchen and eliminated all nut danger that might befall her youngest grandchild.

However, one lonely candy in its shiny golden wrapper had somehow evaded Nana's candy cull. It sat separated from the herd, calling to Nadia, who couldn't resist. As soon as Nana's back was turned, Nadia had popped the deadly morsel into her mouth. For fear she would get into trouble, she initially hid her swelling lips and flushed face, but when she began to struggle for breath, her predicament became obvious. The EpiPen needle came out of its pouch, and an argument ensued about its use. Rather than wasting time with instructions, Poppy piled everyone into the car and drove at breakneck speed to the hospital where Nadia was instantly admitted and put on oxygen and intravenous drip.

Blissfully unaware of our family's emergency excursion, Pieter and I packed our canoe and set off for home. We had consumed much of our supplies and were able to traverse the six-kilometer portage in one trip. Having spent the previous two days sitting on rocks, we took off our life vests and put them under our sore bottoms in the delusional belief we could always grab them if necessary.

To protect his thighs from sun burn, Pieter covered his legs with his shirt and tied the sleeves under his knees to avoid it being blown away during our travel. We were on our final lag of the journey, paddling between two islands. The island on our right was uninhabited, while on our left, a family with three boys waved at us as we passed. We waved back and continued to paddle into the open lake.

The canoe began to rock wildly. We were caught off guard by the gusting wind from which we had been protected seconds before. We struggled to keep the nose pointed into the waves, but without the extra weight of the gear, the canoe was a lot more unstable. We rocked from side to side until both of us got dumped into the lake.

Miraculously, the canoe righted itself and took off in the direction of the two islands.

The cold water came as a shock after having been overheated from sun and the exertion of paddling My first thought was to hang on to my paddle for dear life. First of all, it had been Pieter's anniversary gift and was elaborately carved with an eagle; secondly, it was wood and could float. I hoped that it might be able to hold me up if I needed a break from swimming.

As soon as my head broke through the surface of the water, I looked for Pieter.
The night before, he had told me he didn't consider himself a strong swimmer. And now he had hiking boots on his feet, a shirt tied around his legs, and his life vest was far out of reach. It was floating away in the canoe's wake. After seconds that lasted an eternity, his head broke the surface. The family on the island, having witnessed our predicament, had run to the shoreline. The father and the oldest son jumped into their canoe and set out to capture ours, while the mother had positioned herself where we could see her waving and calling to us.
"Swim—swim to me! You can do it! Keep going!"
It helped.

By the time we got to her, we were barely able to stand. She grabbed our arms and pulled us out of the water. We followed her to the family's campsite where we sat by the fire, exhausted and grateful to be alive. It turned out we had been very lucky, having happened upon a Scout leader and his family.

When we felt somewhat recovered, we checked our packs for dry clothing. Mine, being canvas, left me out of luck, but Pieter's turned out to be waterproof. I dressed in one of his sweaters that hung on me like an oversized dress. It was comforting and warm as was the cup of tea I was offered. We spent two hours with the family, waiting for the wind to die down so we could cross the lake that lay between us and our car. By late afternoon, we said goodbye to our rescuers and set out again. The lake was much calmer, but we were a lot more careful now. From that day forward, we never canoed without wearing life vests.

On our arrival home, Nadia had recovered and was out of the hospital. She was more careful with stray candies from that point on. It was her last visit to a hospital because of an allergic reaction. We had all learned something from our disastrous thirteenth wedding anniversary.

The Backyard Construction Project

As soon as we moved to the country, my mother began lobbying for a swimming pool. She continued for two years and finally agreed to help finance this venture.

It was one of the hottest summers on record, and we couldn't wait to jump into our new pool. With great excitement, we watched the excavation in the backyard. Besides old and broken crockery, we unearthed part of the foundation from a long-forgotten barn.

That summer, we had two young German students staying with us. Both girls were in their early twenties, and I noticed they showed an unprecedented interest in our pool project. When I joined them at the window, I saw that it wasn't the massive hole in the ground that had piqued their interest, but rather the shirtless men pouring cement. My daughters felt compelled to inform their father that I too had taken up post by the window to supervise the pool project.

It wasn't long before Pieter rode past our window on the lawn tractor. When he was sure of an audience, he took off his shirt. This action, however, didn't result in quite the desired reaction. His skin was blindingly white, being rarely exposed to the sun, and he was no longer the lean and muscular guy he had been in his early twenties. Not only did he suffer our mirth, he also gave himself a spectacular sun burn.

Our pool project came to an abrupt halt when our fencing material went on back order. Pieter had taken a three-week vacation from work with the intention of building five hundred feet of fence. Instead, he was on standby, nursing a sunburn.

To our great relief, the fencing material arrived one week before he had to return to work. His sunburn had healed, and he laboured, no longer shirtless, from morning to night under the scorching sun, pulling chain-link fencing.

Our pool crew left after the final layer of cement had been applied. According to municipal by-law, the pool could not be filled until the fence had been installed and inspected. But the big guy in the sky cared little for municipal by-laws and filled our pool with rain water. Once the deluge was over, we had three feet of water, sand, and mud in our pool, which now resembled a pond. When the workers returned to fix the damage, they first had to rescue some ten frogs that had made it their new home.

We had to wait a week before an inspector sanctioned our

new fence and then another for our pool crew to return and install the liner. We watched the water truck fill our pool as we naively planned our first evening dip with great anticipation. However, when we hung the thermometer into the pool, we received a rude awakening. The water must have been shipped from the Arctic because it was barely fourteen degrees Celsius.

Once again, we were forced to wait while the temperature crept up by two degrees per day. While we waited and dreamed of our first family swim, we noticed an increasing number of bees taking a dip in our pool. Apparently, they were not bothered by the cool temperature. Word got around, and before we knew it, we had half a swarm in the pool. We had waited all week for the temperature to rise, and now that it was a balmy twenty-one degrees, we all stood helplessly around the edge of the pool, looking wistfully at the aquamarine water and the hundreds of bees swimming in it.

We knew that there were hives in the fields across the road, but the bees had never bothered us. Now they came to visit in droves. We called around to ascertain whose bees they might be, and finally found the owner of the hives. Once the beekeeper provided a water source for his bees, the number of stinging visitors decreased to a manageable number. Still, nobody felt comfortable jumping in before first checking and double-checking whether the coast was clear, especially after getting stung once or twice.

It wasn't until the following summer that we truly came to enjoy our swimming pool – without frogs or bees.

Head over Heels

It was Maya's last summer before going to university, and she was enjoying some quiet time with both her sisters away at camp. Lucia was an Ontario Ranger for the summer, and Nadia spent a week at Upper Canada Village.

I was going to pick her up and had to leave home by seven o'clock in the morning in order to attend the children's concert by 1:00 p.m. This meant I didn't have enough time to walk Dumbledore, our oversized dog, before my departure.

I woke Maya, who had promised she would look after the dog. She could hardly refuse as we had just bought her a brand-new laptop.
"Wake up, sweetheart. Breakfast is on the table. I'll leave my cell phone on. Please remember to walk Dumbly."
"Okay, Mom. Have a good trip."

At ten thirty, I was just outside Kingston, my phone rang for the first time.
"Mom, how do you clean dog poop off the living room carpet?"
"Oh, Maya! Did you not walk him?"

"No! It's your fault. You didn't wake me!"

"I did."

"Well, I don't remember. Now how do I clean up that Jurassic Park-sized pile of poop?"

I gave her instructions and finished by saying, "I'm soooo glad you're enjoying your new laptop!"

"I love you too, Mom," she said, and hung up.

A few kilometers later, my phone rang again.

"Mom, where are the bandages?"

"Bandages? Are you bleeding?

"Hmmm . . . yes, let's see . . . my elbows, my knees, my foot, and oh, yeah—my boobs!"

"What did you do to yourself?"

"I didn't. It was YOUR dog! I had tied him out back and opened the front door to let out the stench. When I was finally done cleaning the carpet, I went to the kitchen to have breakfast. I had just sat down when YOUR dog kicked the back door. You really need to teach him to bark when he wants in, you know? Anyhow, I let him in, forgetting that I had left the front door open."

Dumbledore had made several successful bids for freedom in the past. The last time, he had made it all the way to the local golf course where he invited himself to dinner on the patio. I had visions of him playing another round at Settlers' Ghost Golf Club.

Dumbledore and Maya both had spotted the open front

door and the gateway to freedom at the same instant. He prepared to jump the three steps that led down to the door just as she threw herself at him with her battle cry of "No, you won't!" and grabbed hold of his fur.

Dumbly leapt, not realizing he was now attached. The force of his sudden take-off separated Maya from her pyjama pants, and she flew, bare-bottomed, through the front door, still clutching the dog.

She fell victim to the laws of physics and the sling-shot effect. When Dumbledore stopped, she kept going, sliding along the stone patio and coming to rest in front of him, still holding him in a head lock.

"Don't worry Mom. I didn't damage your precious stud dog."

"Where is he now?"

"He's lying on his bed, eyeing me with trepidation. I don't think he'll try running for the front door again quite so soon."

Laughter is supposedly therapeutic. Did that make Dumbledore a therapy dog?

By the time Maya headed off to university, both her wounded pride and her scrapes had healed.

Her laptop, however, did not live happily ever after, as laptops never do.

Epilogue and Acknowledgments

Maya was the first to leave home, followed by Lucia one year later. Within a few years, all three daughters had flown the nest. As a parent, you know you've done your job well when your children have the confidence to leave home and strike out on their own.

I want to thank my daughters, Maya, Lucia, and Nadia, for their love, friendship, and the wonderful relationship we enjoy as adults.
My gratitude to my ex-husband, Pieter, for our beautiful daughters and the lifelong friendship we have managed to keep through ups and downs.

Although they've passed on, I would like to thank our respective mothers, Anuschka and Nell, for having taken an active role in raising our children and helping us over the years in so many ways. My gratitude to my entire family for allowing me to share your (mis)adventures with the world at large.

My appreciation also goes to my editor Irene Kavanagh for her keen eyes and invaluable feedback, as well as my niece, Floriana Ehninger-Cuervo, for the cover artwork, and Monika Bernolak for her help with the cover design.

And finally, thank you to my friends and readers for your laughter and tears that make writing worthwhile.

Made in the USA
Middletown, DE
17 January 2020